TRANSLATING THE BIBLE

The Ethiopic Version of the Old Testament

TRANSLATING THE BIBLE

The Ethiopic Version of the Old Testament

Michael A. Knibb, FBA

Samuel Davidson Professor of Old Testament Studies

King's College London

THE SCHWEICH LECTURES
OF THE BRITISH ACADEMY
1995

Published for THE BRITISH ACADEMY
by OXFORD UNIVERSITY PRESS

Oxford University Press, Great Clarendon Street, Oxford OX2 6DP

Oxford New York
Athens Auckland Bangkok Bogota Bombay
Buenos Aires Calcutta Cape Town Dar es Salaam
Delhi Florence Hong Kong Istanbul Karachi
Kuala Lumpur Madras Madrid Melbourne
Mexico City Nairobi Paris Singapore
Taipei Tokyo Toronto Warsaw

and associated companies in
Berlin Ibadan

Published in the United States by
Oxford University Press Inc., New York

British Library Cataloguing in Publication Data
Data available

ISBN 0–19–726194–9

Typeset by the author
Printed in Great Britain
on acid-free paper by
The Cromwell Press Limited
Trowbridge, Wilts

To

Edward Ullendorff, FBA,

Accademico Linceo,

in friendship and gratitude

Contents

Preface

I would like to express my sincere thanks to the members of the Schweich Committee for the very great honour they did me in inviting me to give the Schweich Lectures for 1995. I would also like to record here my gratitude to the Academy for the award earlier in my career of a British Academy Research Readership. Much of the research that lies behind these lectures was undertaken during my tenure of that Readership.

A version of the first lecture was given in October 1998 at a symposium held at the Institut für Afrikanistik und Äthiopistik of the University of Hamburg, and I would like to offer my thanks to Professor Siegbert Uhlig and his colleagues for the warm welcome that they gave to the participants in the symposium.

It was my original intention to publish the lectures more or less in the form in which they were given, apart from the addition of a proper scholarly apparatus, and I had hoped to be able to do this within a year or so of delivering them. In the event commitments within King's College and as a member of the Humanities Research Board, as it then was, meant that there had to be a delay. But the delay has had the advantage that it gave me the opportunity to revise my views slightly in the light of further research, particularly in the case of the first lecture, and to incorporate some additional material. Despite this, what is printed here represents in all essentials the lectures as they were given in November 1995.

It will not escape notice that many of the examples on which I draw in the second and third lectures are taken from the Book of Ezekiel. I have been engaged on the preparation of a critical edition of the Ethiopic text of this book for some time, and that edition will, I trust, provide not only evidence to justify the readings in Ezekiel I have adopted, but also further justification for the general approach reflected in these lectures.

It should be noted that Ethiopia in the context of these lectures refers to the historic entity of Abyssinia in its semitic connotation.

Conventional English spellings have been used for the names of persons and places mentioned in these lectures. Biblical references are given according to the chapter and verse divisions of the Septuagint and follow the Göttingen edition or Rahlfs. A note on the text-editions that have been used is given at the beginning of the bibliography.

The research on which these lectures are based could not have been undertaken without the help provided by the staff of a number of libraries, particularly the British Library, the libraries of King's College London and the School of Oriental and African Studies, and the Bodleian Library, and I would like to express my thanks to them. I would also like to thank Harold Short and his colleagues in the Centre for Computing in the Humanities at King's College London for their advice and support. Amongst members of the staff of the British Academy I would particularly like to thank Rosemary Lambeth for her help at the time the lecures were given, and James Rivington and Janet English for their work in relation to the publication of the lectures.

I am very conscious of the enormous intellectual and personal debt I owe to Edward Ullendorff, and it is a particular pleasure to dedicate these lectures to him. If, in the first lecture, I present a view of the origin of the Ethiopic Bible at variance with his own, I have been led to do so only because of the stimulus provided by his writings and by the questions he himself has posed.

Finally, I wish to thank my wife for her constant encouragement in this as in other enterprises.

King's College London
July 1999   Michael Knibb

Abbreviations

AASF	Annales Academiæ Scientiarum Fennicæ
AF	Äthiopistische Forschungen
BBB	Bonner Biblische Beiträge
BFBS	British and Foreign Bible Society
BSOAS	*Bulletin of the School of Oriental and African Studies*
CSCO	Corpus Scriptorum Christianorum Orientalium
EMML	Ethiopian Manuscript Microfilm Library
GCS	Die griechischen christlichen Schriftsteller der ersten drei Jahrhunderte
JA	*Journal asiatique*
JAOS	*Journal of the American Oriental Society*
JES	*Journal of Ethiopian Studies*
JNES	*Journal of Near Eastern Studies*
JSS	*Journal of Semitic Studies*
MRAL	*Memorie della R. Accademia dei Lincei*
MSU	Mitteilungen des Septuaginta–Unternehmens
PO	Patrologia Orientalis
RE	*Realencyklopädie für protestantische Theologie und Kirche*
RIÉth	Recueil des inscriptions de l'Éthiopie
RRAL	*Rendiconti della R. Accademia dei Lincei*
SC	Sources Chrétiennes
SCS	Septuagint and Cognate Studies
TRE	*Theologische Realenzyklopädie*
VOHD	Verzeichnis der orientalischen Handschriften in Deutschland

ZA	*Zeitschrift für Assyriologie*
ZDMG	*Zeitschrift der Deutschen Morgenländischen Gesellschaft*

Problems and Solutions

I

'Bible Translations' was one of the three main topics considered by Edward Ullendorff in the memorable series of Schweich Lectures that he gave in 1967 under the title *Ethiopia and the Bible*, and in these circumstances an explanation is perhaps required for the decision to devote this series of Schweich Lectures to the Geez translation of the Old Testament, even though this formed only one of the matters with which he was concerned.[1] There can be no doubt of the importance of the Ethiopic Old Testament within the Ethiopian context, an importance which derives from its significance for Ethiopic lexicography, its central role within the corpus of Ethiopic literature, and from the influence which it has exerted on Ethiopian life and culture.[2] In a wider context the Ethiopic version of the Old Testament

---

[1] E. Ullendorff, *Ethiopia and the Bible* (The Schweich Lectures of the British Academy, 1967), London, 1968, 31–62.

[2] For the influence of the Old Testament on Ethiopian life, see E. Ullendorff, 'Hebraic–Jewish Elements in Abyssinian (Monophysite) Christianity', *JSS* 1 (1956), 216–56 (reprinted with additions and corrections in *Studia Aethiopica et Semitica* (AF 24), Stuttgart, 1987, XI–XII, 2–42); id., *Ethiopia and the Bible*, 73–130; cf. Taddesse Tamrat, *Church and State in Ethiopia, 1270–1527* (Oxford Studies in African Affairs), Oxford, 1972, 218–19. Ullendorff (*Ethiopia and the Bible*, 15–30, cf. 10–11) has argued that 'Old Testament influences and reflections had probably reached Ethiopia even before the introduction of Christianity in the fourth century and before the translation of the Bible'; but on the question of the date at which the Old Testament began to have an influence on

is also of importance because it forms part of the history of the transmission of the Old Testament text, and particularly of the Septuagint. And yet much still remains unclear about the origin, history and character of the Old Testament in Geez, and this, it is hoped, is justification enough for returning to this subject. Quite apart from this, research in this field has certainly not stood still over the past thirty years, while Edward Ullendorff himself, both in his Schweich Lectures and in his other writings,[1] has posed a series of questions which demand answers. If, particularly in this first lecture, I argue for views which are at variance with those he has espoused, I do so in full consciousness of the profound debt which all those concerned with Ethiopian studies owe to him, and above all of the debt which I personally owe to him.

The history of the Ethiopic Old Testament is commonly divided into three stages. It is widely believed that the process of translating the Bible into Geez properly began in the fifth century, more than one hundred years after the conversion of the Aksumite kingdom of Ethiopia to Christianity,[2] and that the process was complete by the

---

Ethiopian life, see M. Rodinson, 'Sur la question des "influences juives" en Éthiopie', *JSS* 9 (1964), 11–19, and the comments of Rodinson in *Bibliotheca Orientalis* 21 (1964), 238–45, and in *JSS* 17 (1972), 166–70; H. Brakmann, *Die Einwurzelung der Kirche im spätantiken Reich von Aksum*, Bonn, 1994, 172–85.

[1] See particularly E. Ullendorff, 'An Aramaic "Vorlage" of the Ethiopic Text of Enoch?', *Atti del Convegno Internazionale di Studi Etiopici (Roma, 2–4 aprile 1959)* (Accademia Nazionale dei Lincei, Problemi attuali di scienza e di cultura, Quaderno N. 48), Rome, 1960, 259–68; 'Hebrew, Aramaic and Greek: the Versions underlying Ethiopic Translations of Bible and Intertestamental Literature', in G. Rendsburg et al. (eds), *The Bible World: Essays in Honour of Cyrus H. Gordon*, New York, 1980, 249–57 (reprinted in *Studia Aethiopica et Semitica* (AF 24), Stuttgart, 1987, 43–51); 'Hebrew Elements in the Ethiopic Old Testament', *Jerusalem Studies in Arabic and Islam* 9 (1987), 42–50.

[2] For a recent general account of the Aksumite kingdom, and particularly of its material culture, see D. W. Phillipson, *Ancient Ethiopia. Aksum: Its Antecedents and Successors*, London, 1998. For the conversion of Ethiopia to Christianity, see e.g. Brakmann, *Die*

middle of the seventh century at the latest. There is clear evidence that the Ethiopic translation was made from a Greek text, or at least primarily from a Greek text. It is argued that at a second stage this original translation, the so-called Old Ethiopic, was revised on the basis of Arabic or Syro-Arabic texts to produce what has been termed the 'vulgar recension'. This process of revision is attributed to the mid-fourteenth century, to the literary renaissance that began during the reign of Amda Sion at the time of the 'restoration' of the Solomonic dynasty.[1] Finally, it is argued that in the seond half of the fifteenth century, or a little later, a further revision was undertaken, this time on the basis of the Hebrew text. This revised Ethiopic text represents the so-called academic recension; it is the text found in most of the later manuscripts of the Ethiopic Old Testament and is to a very great extent the text printed in da Bassano's four-volume edition of this version.[2] There are, however, difficulties connected

---

Einwurzelung der Kirche, 51–136; S. Munro-Hay, *Aksum: An African Civilisation of Late Antiquity*, Edinburgh, 1991, 61–103, 196–213; id., *Ethiopia and Alexandria: The Metropolitan Episcopacy of Ethiopia* (Bibliotheca nubica et aethiopica 5), Warsaw and Wiesbaden, 1997, 58–66.

[1] For the end of the Zagwe dynasty, the assumption of power by Yekuno Amlak (1270–85), and the reign of Amda Zion (1314–44), see Taddesse Tamrat, *Church and State in Ethiopia*, 60–68, 72–118, 132–45. For the literary renaissance that began in the reign of Amda Sion, see I. Guidi, *Storia della letteratura etiopica*, Rome, 1932, 24–49.

[2] F. da Bassano (ed.), ብሉይ፡ ኪዳን፡ , 4 vols, Asmara, 1922/3–1925/6. Da Bassano's edition of the Ethiopic Old Testament was the first to be published in Ethiopia and remains the most important. It does not provide a critical edition of the text, but was intended as a practical tool for the use of Ethiopian clergy and laity. See the review by O. Löfgren ('Die äthiopische Bibelausgabe der katholische Mission, mit einer Kollation des Danieltextes,' *Monde Oriental* 23 (1929), 174–80) and the comments of Ullendorff (*Ethiopia and the Bible*, 59–60). See also M. A. Knibb, 'Hebrew and Syriac Elements in the Ethiopic Version of Ezekiel?', *JSS* 33 (1988), 12–14.

with all three stages of the history I have just outlined and it is with these that I shall be primarily concerned in this lecture.[1]

II

In the course of his Schweich Lectures Edward Ullendorff had occasion more than once to draw attention to the difficulty of reaching firm conclusions because of the absence of adequate preliminary work.[2] In some respects at least the situation has improved over the last thirty years, and it is appropriate to begin by noting briefly what has been achieved. Perhaps the most important factor in the improved situation has been the increase in the availability of manuscripts that are old by Ethiopian standards in consequence of various projects to microfilm manuscripts in Ethiopia. The most important of these in terms of its size was undoubtedly the American-sponsored Ethiopian Manuscript Microfilm Library (EMML) project, under whose auspices over seven and a half thousand manuscripts were photographed.[3] While many of these manuscripts were recent in date

---

[1] For more details of the history outlined above and bibliographical references, see Knibb, *JSS* 33 (1988), 14–17. Most of those who in the present century have worked on the Ethiopic version of the Old Testament, or have produced editions of books of the Ethiopic Old Testament, have adopted the view outlined above, albeit with some differences: see A. Heider, *Die aethiopische Bibelübersetzung*, Leipzig, 1902, 5; J. Schäfers, *Die äthiopische Übersetzung des Propheten Jeremias*, Freiburg im Breisgau, 1912, VII–VIII, 27–71; O. Löfgren, *Die äthiopische Übersetzung des Propheten Daniel*, Paris, 1927, XXXVIII–L; H. F. Fuhs, *Die äthiopische Übersetzung des Propheten Micha* (BBB 28), Bonn, 1968, 31–8; id., *Die äthiopische Übersetzung des Propheten Hosea* (BBB 38), Bonn, 1971, 103–22. See also S. P. Brock, 'Bibelübersetzungen I. 8: Die Übersetzungen ins Äthiopische. 2: Altes Testament' *TRE* 6 (1980), 206–7.

[2] Ullendorff, *Ethiopia and the Bible*, 31, 34, 36, 55.

[3] Cf. W. Harrelson and J. G. Plante in Getatchew Haile and W. F. Macomber, *A Catalogue of Ethiopian Manuscripts microfilmed for the Ethiopian Manuscript Microfilm*

and routine in character, a number of manuscripts, particularly from outside Addis Ababa, that either were old or contained rare or unique texts were microfilmed, and a start has been made in putting these to good use.[1] Prior to this the late Professor Ernst Hammerschmidt had photographed one hundred and eighty-two manuscripts belonging to important ancient monasteries in the Lake Tana region,[2] and Dr Donald Davies had photographed thirty-five old manuscripts, including three valuable manuscripts of the gospels belonging to the monastery of Abba Garima.[3]

Library, Addis Ababa, and for the Hill Monastic Manuscript Library, Collegeville, vol. V, Collegeville, Minnesota, 1981, v; information about the progress of the project was given in the prefaces to the previous volumes of the catalogue. See also Macomber, 'Two New Projects for Microfilming Oriental Manuscripts', in W. Voigt (ed.), *XVIII. Deutscher Orientalistentag vom 1. bis 5. Oktober 1972 in Lübeck: Vorträge* (ZDMG Supplement II), Wiesbaden, 1974, 82–84; id., 'The Present State of the Microfilm Collection of the Ethiopian Manuscript Microfilm Library', in G. Goldenberg (ed.), *Ethiopian Studies: Proceedings of the Sixth International Conference, Tel Aviv, 14–17 April 1980*, Rotterdam, 1986, 389–96.

[1] See e.g. O. Raineri, *Atti di Habta Mâryâm (†1497) e di Iyâsu (†1508), Santi Monaci Etiopici* (Orientalia Christiana Analecta 235), Rome, 1990; Getatchew Haile and Misrak Amare, *Beauty of the Creation* (ሥን ፡ ፍጥረት ፡) (JSS Monograph 16), Manchester, 1991; Getatchew Haile, *The Mariology of Emperor Zär'a Ya'eqob of Ethiopia* (Orientalia Christiana Analecta 242), Rome, 1992.

[2] For a report on the project, see E. Hammerschmidt, *Äthiopische Handschriften vom Tânâsee 1: Reisebericht und Beschreibung der Handschriften in dem Kloster des heiligen Gabriel auf der Insel Kebrân* (VOHD XX/1), Wiesbaden, 1973, 41–81.

[3] For a brief report on his visit to Ethiopia and a list of the dated manuscripts, see D. M. Davies, 'The Dating of Ethiopic Manuscripts', *JNES* 46 (1987), 287–88. The Abba Garima manuscripts are almost certainly the oldest Ethiopic manuscripts that are known, but Davies's view (see pp. 288–307 of his article) that they date back to between the eighth century and the tenth is not supported by the palaeographical evidence. Similarly, there are no verifiable criteria for Macomber's view that they date from the tenth and eleventh centuries (Macomber, *Catalogue of Ethiopian Manuscripts from Abbâ Garimâ*

The importance of this work of microfilming can be observed in the editions of biblical texts that have been published since the early 70s. Thus for his recently published study of the Ethiopic text of the synoptic gospels and his edition of the Ethiopic version of Mark,[1] Zuurmond examined some two hundred and fifty manuscripts, of which more than three fifths were available only as a result of the microfilming projects just mentioned. Of the manuscripts available from these microfilming projects, no less than five[2] are older than Bibliothèque Nationale Éth. 22 (Zotenberg, No. 32), on which

---

(below, p. 8, n. 2), 1–11). For the date of the Abba Garima manuscripts, see further below, p. 6, n. 2.

[1] R. Zuurmond, *Novum Testamentum aethiopice: The Synoptic Gospels*. Part I: *General Introduction*. Part II: *Edition of the Gospel of Mark* (AF 27), Stuttgart, 1989. See on this Knibb, *BSOAS* 55 (1992), 124–26.

[2] Abba Garima I, Abba Garima III, Abba Garima II, Lalibala — Madhane 'Alam (= EMML 6907), EMML 1832. For the dates of these manuscripts, see Zuurmond, *Novum Testamentum aethiopice: The Synoptic Gospels*. Part I, 63; Part II, 44–56; S. Uhlig, *Äthiopische Paläographie* (AF 22), Stuttgart, 1988, 48, 102–104, 116–18, 144–76. The lack of sufficient comparative material makes it impossible to date the above manuscripts precisely, but it is almost certain that Abba Garima I, Abba Garima III, and the Lalibala gospel manuscript go back to the Zagwe period and antedate the restoration of the Solomonic dynasty in 1270. The *terminus ad quem* of Abba Garima I and Abba Garima III can be placed in the thirteenth cenury, but both are probably older, and Abba Garima I has been dated by Uhlig (p. 176) to the twelfth century or the beginning of the thirteenth. The Lalibala manuscript is dated to the reign of Lalibala, which is traditionally attributed to the period 1140–1180. The colophon mentioning the king may have been copied from an older manuscript, but even so the manuscript can be dated at the latest in the thirteenth century and may very well go back to the second half of the twelfth. All three manuscripts appear on palaeographical grounds to be somewhat older than any other manuscript from the period. As to the two others, Abba Garima II can be dated to the end of the thirteenth century or the beginning of the fourteenth. EMML 1832 is dated to 1280/1281, and even if it is younger than this, in Zuurmond's view (Part II, p. 55) it is only younger by a few decades.

Hackspill's study of the Ethiopic text of the gospels, the most important prior to that of Zuurmond, was based;[1] and of these five, three — Abba Garima I, Abba Garima III, and the gospel manuscript from Lalibala — almost certainly antedate the restoration of the Solomonic dynasty in 1270 and are the oldest Ethiopic manuscripts that are known.[2] In a similar way, five of the eight older manuscripts used by Uhlig and Maehlum for their 1993 edition of the Captivity Epistles[3] were accessible only as a result of the microfilming projects. In the sphere of the Pseudepigrapha, Lake Tana 9 from the monastery of St Gabriel on Kebran, which was photographed by Professor Hammerschmidt in 1968, was used by me in my edition of Enoch[4] and has been used in all recent translations of the book; it was also used by VanderKam for his edition and translation of Jubilees.[5] In the Old Testament sphere, Fuhs was not able to make use of any of the newly-available manuscripts for his editions of Micah and Hosea

---

[1] L. Hackspill, 'Die äthiopische Evangelienübersetzung (Math. I–X)', *ZA* 11 (1896), 117–96, 367–88. Hackspill argued (pp. 127–29, 159) that BN Éth. 22 dated from the thirteenth century — so already Guidi and Zotenberg — and was of particular importance because all other manuscripts of the Ethiopic text of the gospels that were known to him dated from the fifteenth century or later. However, S. Grébaut ('L'age du ms. éth. n° 32 de Paris (Bibliothèque Nationale)', *Aethiops* 4 (1931), 9–11) more plausibly argued that it dates from the second half of the fourteenth century, and Uhlig (*Äthiopische Paläographie*, 249–51) believes that even this date may be too early.

[2] For the dates of Abba Garima I, Abba Garima III, and the Lalibala manuscript, see above, p. 6, n. 2.

[3] S. Uhlig and H. Maehlum, *Novum Testamentum aethiopice: Die Gefangenschaftsbriefe* (AF 33), Stuttgart, 1993. The manuscripts are EMML 6462, Lake Tana 110, Lake Tana 139, EMML 7333, EMML 2198. See on this edition Knibb, *BSOAS* 59 (1996), 203–205.

[4] M. A. Knibb with the assistance of E. Ullendorff, *The Ethiopic Book of Enoch: A new edition in the light of the Aramaic Dead Sea Fragments.* Vol. 1: *Text and Apparatus*; Vol. 2: *Introduction, Translation and Commentary*, Oxford, 1978.

[5] J. C. VanderKam, *The Book of Jubilees.* Vol. 1: *Critical Text*; Vol. 2: *Translation* (CSCO 510–511), Leuven, 1989.

published in 1967 and 1971,[1] and no other Old Testament text has been published since. But my own forthcoming edition of Ezekiel is certainly dependent to a considerable extent on these 'new' manuscripts.

The exploitation of these newly microfilmed manuscripts has been facilitated by the fairly prompt publication of catalogues of the three collections. The privately published catalogue of the Davies manuscripts by Macomber[2] has to be regarded in some respects as provisional, but we are on firmer ground with the fine catalogue of the Lake Tana manuscripts by Professor Hammerschmidt, of which two of the projected three volumes appeared before his death,[3] and with the as yet incomplete multi-volume catalogue of the EMML manuscripts, which was begun by Macomber but is now the sole responsibility of Getatchew Haile.[4] The EMML catalogue is not conceived along the lines of the classic works of scholars such as Dillmann and Wright. But in the form which it has possessed since the fifth volume, according to which only manuscripts that can be regarded as important are given a full description, the EMML catalogue is a very useful working tool, and certainly the ten volumes

---

[1] For these editions, see above, p. 4, n. 1.

[2] W. F. Macomber, *Catalogue of Ethiopian Manuscripts from Abbâ Garimâ, Asatan (Church of St. Mary), Axum (Church of Zion) ... from microfilms in the collection of Dr. Donald Davies, De Land, Florida and Godfrey, Ontario, and of the Hill Monastic Manuscript Library, St. John's University, Collegeville, Minnesota*, Privately reproduced, Collegeville, Minnesota, 1979.

[3] E. Hammerschmidt, *Äthiopische Handschriften vom Tânâsee 1* (see above, p. 5, n. 2); id., *Äthiopische Handschriften vom Tânâsee 2: Die Handschriften von Dabra Mâryâm und von Rêmâ* (VOHD XX/2), Wiesbaden, 1977.

[4] W. F. Macomber and Getatchew Haile, *A Catalogue of Ethiopian Manuscripts microfilmed for the Ethiopian Manuscript Microfilm Library, Addis Ababa, and for the Hill Monastic Manuscript Library, Collegeville*, vol. I–, Collegeville, Minnesota, 1975–. For details of the individual volumes, see the bibliography.

prepared by Macomber and by Getatchew Haile represent a notable achievement.

During the last thirty years excellent catalogues have also been issued of a number of European collections of Ethiopian manuscripts that had never, or only partially, been catalogued previously. These works, which are of a quite different order to the EMML catalogues just described, have covered the collections in London (Strelcyn), Manchester (Strelcyn), Uppsala (Löfgren), Berlin (Hammerschmidt and Six), Munich (Six and Hammerschmidt), other libraries in Germany (Six and Hammerschmidt), and the Conti Rossini collection in Rome (Strelcyn).[1]

The credibility of any study of the history of a text is dependent on the credibility of the dates assigned to the manuscripts that are used, and in this respect there are particular problems associated with the study of Ethiopian texts. The majority of Ethiopic manuscripts are undated, and the dates contained in the small nunber of dated manuscripts (some ten to fifteen per cent of the total[2]) have to be treated with caution. It is well known that the physical appearance of Ethiopic manuscripts provides no guide to their age because of the poor conditions in which manuscripts have often been kept in Ethiopia. Palaeographical critera provide the only relatively certain means of dating Ethiopic manuscripts, but even here there are many uncertainties which arise from our ignorance of such factors as whether the copyist was influenced by purely local traditions, or whether he was trying to imitate the ductus of the manuscript he was copying.

The importance of these issues can be illustrated positively by the work of Zuurmond, whose convincing reconstruction of the complex history of the Ethiopic text of the gospels[3] is to a very great extent based on a careful dating of the relevant manuscripts. The

---

[1] For details, see the bibliography under the name of the cataloguer.

[2] Cf. Uhlig, *Äthiopische Paläographie*, 61.

[3] Zuurmond, *Novum Testamentum aethiopice: The Synoptic Gospels*. Part I, 37–137.

importance of these issues can also be illustrated negatively by reference to the exaggerated claims made for one of the Old Testament manuscripts microfilmed by the EMML project, EMML 2080. Shortly after the manuscript was microfilmed the claim was made that this was 'the oldest known Ethiopian Old Testament manuscript in the world' and that it was to be dated, on the basis of its script, to the twelfth or thirteenth century. The discovery was held to be of particular significance because of the large number of Old Testament books the manuscript contained.[1] If the date originally assigned to the manuscript had been sound, the discovery would indeed have been of major significance. But a more considered view of its script indicates that the manuscript belongs in the second half of the fifteenth century or the first half of the sixteenth,[2] and while the manuscript is still of importance and interest, it certainly does not have the textual significance that was originally claimed for it.[3]

In view of the circumstances just described, it is perhaps surprising that until very recently there was no comprehensive treatment of Ethiopic palaeography, and scholars were forced to rely

---

[1] W. Harrelson and J. G. Plante in W. F. Macomber, *A Catalogue of Ethiopian Manuscripts microfilmed for the Ethiopian Manuscript Microfilm Library*, vol. III, iv; cf. Macomber, 'The Present State of the Microfilm Collection', 393–94. The manuscript contains the Ethiopic text of the prophetic and wisdom books of the Old Testament, and of the books of Enoch, Judith and Esther.

[2] Cf. Uhlig, *Äthiopische Paläographie*, 41, 419–20. According to Sergew Hable Selassie, EMML 2080 dates fom the fifteenth century (cf. Getatchew Haile in Getatchew Haile and W. F. Macomber, *A Catalogue of Ethiopian Manuscripts microfilmed for the Ethiopian Manuscript Microfilm Library*, vol. VI, 147).

[3] Thus in the case of the book of Ezekiel, its text is very similar to that of the Berlin manuscript of the prophetic books (Berlin Peterm. II, Nachtr. 42) that was used by Dillmann and by Cornill more than a century ago.

on the brief surveys provided by Wright[1] and by Conti Rossini,[2] and on the occasional observations on palaeographical matters made by such scholars as Dillmann, Grébaut and Strelcyn. This situation changed significantly in 1988 with the publication of Uhlig's substantial volume on Ethiopic palaeography.[3] Uhlig has divided Ethiopic writing from the eleventh/twelfth century to the present day into eight periods and has provided soundly-based criteria for assigning manuscripts to one or other of these. Whatever differences of view there may be over points of detail, the framework and the criteria provided by Uhlig have placed Ethiopic paleography — and in consequence Ethiopic textual studies — on a much more secure footing.

It is in the light of the work that I have just described that I would like to take up the questions concerning the origin and history of the Ethiopic Old Testament to which I alluded earlier.

III

The account given by Rufinus of the conversion of Ethiopia to Christianity attributes the conversion to the activities of the two captured Tyrian boys, Frumentius, who was subsequently ordained by Athanasius as the first bishop of Ethiopia, and his brother Aedesius.[4]

---

[1] W. Wright, *Catalogue of the Ethiopic Manuscripts in the British Museum acquired since the year 1847*, London, 1877, X–XIII and plates 1–13.

[2] C. Conti Rossini, 'Notice sur les manuscrits éthiopiens de la collection d'Abbadie', *JA* x.19 (1912), 553–65.

[3] S. Uhlig, *Äthiopische Paläographie* (see above, p. 6, n. 2). See the reviews by Ullendorff (*JSS* 36 (1991), 128–34) and Knibb (*ZDMG* 141 (1991), 405–408).

[4] Rufinus, *Historia ecclesiastica* X.9–10 (E. Schwartz and T. Mommsen, *Eusebius Werke* (GCS), II.2, Leipzig, 1908, 972–73; cf. P. R. Amidon, *The Church History of Rufinus of Aquileia, Books 10 and 11*, New York, 1997, 18–20, 46–47). The story is repeated in a number of patristic sources; for details, see Brakmann, *Die Einwurzelung der Kirche im*

The account is not devoid of legendary features, but whatever historical reality lies behind it, the existence of Frumentius is confirmed by the reference to him in the letter, quoted by Athanasius,[1] from Constantius II to the Aksumite rulers.[2] In any event the Christian language and Christian symbolism of the inscriptions and coins of the Aksumite ruler Ezana provide clear evidence for the adoption of Christianity by Ezana as the official religion of the Aksumite kingdom,[3] probably about the middle of the fourth century.[4] However,

---

spätantiken Reich von Aksum, 58–67. The Ethiopian account in the Homily in honour of Frumentius, from which the compiler of the version of the story in the Synaxarium took his information, was based on the version given by Socrates (*Historia Ecclesiastica* I.19; R. Hussey, *Socratis Scholastici Ecclesiastica Historia*, vol. 1, Oxford, 1853, 113-17); see Getatchew Haile, 'The Homily in Honour of St. Frumentius, Bishop of Axum', *Analecta Bollandiana* 97 (1979), 309–18; Sir E. A. Wallis Budge, *The Book of the Saints of the Ethiopian Church*, vol. iv, Cambridge, 1928, 1164–65.

[1] Athanasius, *Apologia ad Constantium* 31 (J.-M. Szymusiak, *Athanase d'Alexandrie: Deux apologies: à l'Empereur Constance; pour sa fuite* (SC 56bis), Paris, 1987, 158–63).

[2] Cf. Zuurmond, *Novum Testamentum aethiopice: The Synoptic Gospels.* Part I, 129, n. 72: 'Although Frumentius is beyond doubt a true person (he figures in Athanasius' correpsondence with the emperor Constantius II) I would not attach too much direct historical value to the charming but highly legendary story of Ethiopia's conversion through the little Frumentius and his brother Edesius, as told by Rufinus.'

[3] For the Christian inscriptions of Ezana (RIÉth 189, 190, 271), see E. Bernand, A. J. Drewes, R. Schneider, F. Anfray, *Recueil des inscriptions de l'Éthiopie des périodes pré-axoumite et axoumite*, Paris, 1991, tome I, 262–71, 370–72; tome II, planches 119–28, 181; for the coins, see recently Munro-Hay, *Aksum: An African Civilisation of Late Antiquity*, 76–78, 189–91, 202. See also Brakmann, *Die Einwurzelung der Kirche*, 67–77.

[4] This dating is based on the view that the ordination of Frumentius by Athanaisus is to be placed after the second return of the latter to Alexandria in 346; cf. Brakmann, *Die Einwurzelung der Kirche*, 58–60, n. 300, 77; Taddesse Tamrat, *Church and State in Ethiopia*, 22, n. 5.

it is likely that Christianity did not at first spread very far beyond the circles of the royal court and the resident merchant classes, and according to Ethiopian tradition it was not until the arrival in Ethiopia of groups of monks from 'Rome', that is from the Eastern Empire, who acted as missionaries that Christianity began to be established more widely in the Aksumite kingdom. The Ethiopian hagiographical traditions[1] refer to two distinct groups of monks, the so–called Nine Saints[2] and the Ṣadqan,[3] as well as to isolated individuals,[4] and place

---

[1] For these traditions, see particularly C. Conti Rossini, *Storia d'Etiopia. Parte prima: Dalle origini all'avvento della Dinastia Salomonide*, Bergamo, 1928, 156–63, pl. LIV; cf. Sergew Hable Sellassie, *Ancient and Medieval Ethiopian History to 1270*, Addis Ababa, 1972, 115–21, 125–26; Brakmann, *Die Einwurzelung der Kirche*, 125–36.

[2] The most important traditions concerning the Nine Saints are preserved in the Gadla Aragawi (Guidi, 'Il "Gadla 'Aragâwi"', *MRAL*, ser. v, vol. 2 (1894 (1896)), 54–96), the Gadla Pantalewon (Conti Rossini, *Vitae sanctorum antiquiorum. I: Acta Yared et Pantalewon* (CSCO, Script. Aeth. ii.17, Textus, Versio), Rome, 1904), the homily on Garima (Conti Rossini, 'L'omilia di Yohannes, vescovo d'Aksum, in onore di Garimâ', *Actes du onzième congrès international des orientalistes, Paris — 1897*, Quatrième section, Paris, 1898, 139–77), and the Gadla Afse (Conti Rossini, 'La leggenda di Abbâ Afsê in Etiopia', *Mélanges Syriens offerts à Monsieur René Dussaud ... par ses amis et ses élèves*, vol. i, Paris, 1939, 151–56; cf. Sergew Hable Selassie, 'New Historical Elements in the "Gedle Aftse"', *JSS* 9 (1964), 200–203).

[3] For the traditions concerning the Ṣadqan, see Conti Rossini, 'Il gadla Sâdqân', *Ricordi di un soggiorno in Eritrea*, fasc. I, Asmara, 1903, V, 7–22; Raineri, '"Gadla Ṣadqan" o "Vita dei Giusti": Missionari dell'Etiopia nel sesto secolo', *Nikolaus* 6 (1978), 143–63; id., '"Vita dei Giusti". Missionari dell'Etiopia nel sesto secolo: varianti e inno,' *Ephemerides Carmeliticae* 31 (1980), 377–413; cf. R. Schneider, 'Une page du Gadla Sâdqân', *Annales d'Éthiopie* 5 (1963), 167–69. See also Getatchew Haile, 'A Text on the Saints of Kädiḥ', in Taddese Beyene (ed.), *Proceedings of the Eighth International Conference of Ethiopian Studies, University of Addis Ababa, 1984*, vol. 1, Addis Ababa, 1988, 653–64.

[4] The isolated individuals include Mattâ' or Libanos, and Yohanni; for the former, cf. Conti Rossini, 'Il gadla Libânos', *Ricordi di un soggiorno in Eritrea*, fasc. I, V–VI, 23–

their activities in the reigns of kings who belong in the latter part of
the fifth century and the first part of the sixth. It has often been argued
that these monks were monophysites who fled to Ethiopia to escape
persecution after the Council of Chalcedon in 451, but it has also been
suggested that the Aksumite kings may have officially encouraged
them to come to Ethiopia.[1]

The earliest clear evidence for the existence of a translation into
Geez of at least some parts of the Bible is provided by the occurrence
of brief quotations from the Psalms, and from one or two other books,
in three royal inscriptions that date from the first half of the sixth
century.[2] But we have no precise knowledge about the time at which,
or the circumstances in which, the translation was undertaken. It is
plausible to assume that the individual books would not have been
translated all at the same time, but only over a period of time, and it is
likely that the first books to be translated would have been the gospels
and the Psalter. It is possible that the translation was begun soon after
the adoption of Christianity by Ezana in the mid-fourth century.[3] But
we have no documentary evidence for this, and it has been argued that
there would not have been an immediate need for an Ethiopic version
of the scriptures in the limited circles in which Christianity was first
established. A majority of scholars would thus now attribute the

---

41; Strelcyn, *Catalogue des manuscrits éthiopiens de l'Accademia Nazionale*, 90–100;
Getatchew Haile, 'The Homily of Abba Eleyas, Bishop of Aksum, on Mätta'', *Analecta
Bollandiana* 108 (1990), 29–47.

[1] Cf. Taddesse Tamrat, *Church and State in Ethiopia*, 29–30.

[2] For these quotations, see Appendix I.

[3] A. Dillmann, for example, attributed the translation to the fourth–fifth century
('Äthiopische Bibelübersetzung', *RE*[2] I (1877), 203: 'in den ersten Zeiten der
Verbreitung des Christentums in Abyssinien, also im 4.–5. Jahrh.); for other scholars
who attributed the translation to this period, see Knibb, *JSS* 33 (1988), 14–15, n. 13. See
also O. Löfgren, 'The Necessity of a Critical Edition of the Ethiopian Bible', in
*Proceedings of the Third International Conference of Ethiopian Studies, Addis Ababa,
1966*, vol. 2, Addis Ababa, 1970, 159–60.

translation of the Bible to the time of the expansion of Christianity in the latter part of the fifth century as a result of the activity of the Nine Saints and other groups of monks. According to Conti Rossini, who was relying on a tradition in the version of the Gadla Libânos that he edited, Mattâ' (Libanos) translated the Gospel of Matthew,[1] and it is widely assumed that the Nine Saints, or other similar groups of missionaries, were responsible for the translation of the scriptures.[2] In this connection the argument, developed by Guidi and Conti Rossini in particular,[3] that these missionaries were Syrians has assumed significance. Thus the attribution of the translation of the scriptures to Syrian missionaries has sometimes been linked to the view that the *Vorlage* of the Old Testament was the Lucianic recension of the Septuagint,[4] while — specifically in relation to the New Testament —

[1] Conti Rossini, *Storia d'Etiopia*, 157–58, 223. For the tradition linking Mattâ' (Libânos) with Matthew, see Conti Rossini, *Ricordi di un soggiorno in Eritrea*, fasc. I, 26; but see below, pp. 23–24. For Mattâ', see also Conti Rossini, 'L'evangelo d'oro di Dabra Libânos', *RRAL*, ser. v, vol. 10 (1901), 177, 184–86.

[2] This view was held, for example, by Guidi (*Storia della letteratura etiopica*, 12–13) and by Conti Rossini (*Storia d'Etiopia*, 223); for other scholars who attributed the translation to this period, see Knibb, *JSS* 33 (1988), 15, n. 14. Cf. Taddesse Tamrat, *Church and State in Ethiopia*, 24: 'No doubt the first thing these Syrian monks set out to do was to translate the Bible and other religious books into Ethiopic.' W. Witakowski ('Syriac Influences in Ethiopian Culture', *Orientalia Suecana* 28–29 (1989–90), 198) states that Syrians 'participated in translating the Bible'; but on p. 193 he notes that it is not clear whether evidence of Syriac influence on the Old Testament reflects the use of the Peshitta or later revision of the Ethiopic on the basis of the Syro–Arabic version.

[3] For details, see below, pp. 25–29.

[4] For this view, see Heider, *Die aethiopische Bibelübersetzung*, 5–6, 9–16; E. Littmann, 'Geschichte des äthiopische Litteratur', in C. Brockelmann et al., *Geschichte der christlichen Litteraturen des Orients* (Die Litteraturen des Ostens in Einzeldarstellungen vii.2), Leipzig, 1907, 223–24; Guidi, *Storia della letteratura etiopica*, 13: 'e che ad essi [the Nine Saints] o ai loro discepoli si debba la traduzione della Sacra Scrittura e nominatamente dei Vangeli, si può inferire dal fatto che il testo in essa seguito non è già

Vööbus argued that the natural assumption must be that Syrian monks would use Syriac, rather than Greek, manuscripts as the basis of their translation.[1] More cautiously Edward Ullendorff has stated: 'the evidence certainly encourages the opinion that, with the advent of

---

quello de Esichio, ricevuto nel Patriarcato alessandrino ... ma bensì il siro-occidentale di S. Luciano, ricevuto nel vasto Patriarcato di Antiochia ed oltre.' (For the misunderstanding inherent in the use of 'siro-occidentale', see H. J. Polotsky, 'Aramaic, Syriac, and Ge'ez', *JSS* 9 (1964), 7–10.) More tentatively, Conti Rossini (*Storia d'Etiopia*, 223) suggested that some books of the Old Testament, such as 3 Ezra, Jeremiah and Amos, may be based on the Lucianic recension. However, so far as Jeremiah is concerned, Heider's view of dependence on the Lucianic recension was decisively, and rightly, rejected by Schäfers (*Die äthiopische Übersetzung des Propheten Jeremias*, VII–VIII, 154–55; cf. J. Ziegler (*Septuaginta. Vetus Testamentum Graecum Auctoritate Academiae Scientiarum Gottingensis editum*. Vol. XV: *Ieremias, Baruch, Threni, Epistula Ieremiae*, 2. Auflage, Göttingen, 1976, 33).

[1] A. Vööbus, *Early Versions of the New Testament: Manuscript Studies* (Papers of the Estonian Theological Society in Exile 6), Stockholm, 1954, 246–65, especially 254–57; cf. id., *Die Spuren eines älteren äthiopischen Evangelientextes im Lichte der literarischen Monumente* (Papers of the Estonian Theological Society in Exile 2), Stockholm, 1951, in which he argued that the hagiographical texts preserved original readings from the Ethiopic version of the gospels, which had disappeared from the biblical manuscripts, and that these original readings were dependent on the Old Syriac version of the gospels. W. W. Müller ('Zwei weitere Bruchstuecke der Aethiopischen Inschrift aus Mârib', *Neue Ephemeris für Semitische Epigraphik* 1 (1972), 70) has suggested — with reference to the reading በልሳንየ ፡ (Old Greek υπο την γλωσσαν μου; Syr ܠܫܢܝ) in Ps. 65:17 (MT 66:17) — that the argument put forward by Vööbus might also apply in the case of the Old Testament: 'Vielleicht lassen sich bei einer eingehenden Untersuchung der frühesten äthiopischen Textzeugen des Alten Testaments ebenfalls noch mehrere Übereinstimmungen mit möglichen syrischen Vorlagen ausfinding machen.' But see the cogent criticisms by Zuurmond (*Novum Testamentum aethiopice: The Synoptic Gospels*. Part I, 119–23, 125–26) both of the methodology of Vööbus and of his discussion of the textual evidence.

Syrian missionaries in the fifth and sixth centuries, Syriac translations were employed in conjunction with the Greek text.'[1]

We shall need to discuss further the view that the translation of the scriptures into Geez is to be attributed to Syrian missionaries. But it may be said straightaway that in the absence of any very substantial or reliable external evidence about the date of the translation and the circumstances in which it was made, views such as the above regarding the *Vorlage* of the Ethiopic version can only be tested against the evidence of the texts themselves. But we are here faced with the difficulty that, apart from the few brief quotations from the Bible that occur in the inscriptions, there is an enormous gap between the date of the translation and the date of the manuscripts that we possess. The translation of the scriptures into Geez was completed at the latest by the mid-seventh century,[2] but it may have been

---

[1] Ullendorff, *Ethiopia and the Bible*, 56.

[2] This view is based on the consideration that with the decline of the Aksumite kingdom, which was well under way in the early part of the seventh century, the circumstances no longer existed in which translation of the scriptures, particularly translation from Greek, is likely. The decline was caused in the first instance by the damage inflicted on Aksum's trade in the Red Sea, and thus on its prosperity, as a result of the Persian conquest of South Arabia and Egypt, and ultimately by the rise of Islam. It was accompanied by a deterioration in the Greek used in the inscriptions on the coins, which indicates that there was a decline in the knowledge of Greek; the issuing of coins appears to have ended in the early part of the seventh century. Cf. Munro-Hay, *Aksum: An African Civilisation of Late Antiquity*, 58, 93–94, 194–95, 258–64. — Support for the view that the translation was completed by no later than the middle of the seventh century is provided by the use of ፍርስ፡ to render Χαλδαῖοι in some passages (e.g. Isa. 43:14; Dan. 3:48) in that it suggests that Persia was at the time still a dominant power; cf. Schäfers, *Die äthiopische Übersetzung des Propheten Jeremias*, 181; Conti Rossini, *Storia d'Etiopia*, 223; Löfgren, *Daniel*, XLVIII. — It has sometimes been asserted, for example by Littmann ('Geschichte des äthiopische Litteratur', 203) and by Conti Rossini (*Storia d'Etiopia*, 223; cf. id.,'Sulla versione e sulla revisione delle sacre scritture in etiopico', ZA 10 (1895), 236, n. 3), on the basis of colophons in Paris BN Éth. 9 (Zotenberg, no. 6) and

completed considerably earlier if the view of Zuurmond is correct that
the report of Cosmas Indicopleustes concerning the flourishing state
of Christianity in the Aksumite kingdom[1] makes it likely that a more
or less completely translated Bible existed by the first quarter of the
sixth century.[2] On the other hand almost all the manuscripts of the
Old Testament in Geez that we possess date from the fifteenth century
or later. There are a small number of fourteenth century manuscripts
such as the Vatican manuscript of the books of Samuel and Kings
(Vat. Borg. Aeth. 3), which is dated to the reign of Amda Sion (1314–
1344) and may be slightly older, or the Oxford manuscript of the
Minor Prophets (Oxford Bodl. Aeth. d. 12 (Dillmann, no. VIII)) and
the Paris manuscript of Daniel and Job (Paris BN Éth. 11 (Zotenberg,
no. 7)), which both probably date from about 1350.[3] But to my
knowledge there are no thirteenth century Ethiopic Old Testament
manuscripts, and certainly none as old as the Abba Garima
manuscripts of the gospels. There is thus a gap of some seven hundred
years, and possibly considerably longer, between the translation of the
Old Testament into Geez and the date of the manuscripts. We have no
knowledge of the vicissitudes suffered by the Ethiopic text during this
period, but it does appear that in the case of the majority of even the

---

Frankfurt Ms. orient. Rüpp. II, 7, that Ecclesiasticus was translated into Geez in 678 and
was one of the last books to be translated. But it is more likely that the colophons were
copied slavishly from an ancestor of the two manuscripts, and that the original colophon
referred to the year in which the ancestor was copied out; but the year given (678) is
problematic and uncertain. See A. Rahlfs, 'Die äthiopische Bibelübersetzung',
Septuaginta–Studien I–III, 2. Auflage, Göttingen, 1965, 679–81; cf. E. Cerulli, *Storia
della letteratura etiopica*, Milan, 1956, 24; Knibb, *JSS* 33 (1988), 15, n. 15.

[1] Cosmas Indicopleustes (*Christian Topography* III.64–66; W. Wolska–Conus, *Cosmas
Indicopleustès: Topographie chrétienne*, tome I (SC 141), Paris, 1968, 502–07) included
Ethiopia among the countries in which 'everywhere there are churches of Christians,
bishops, martyrs, solitary monks, whereby the gospel of Christ is proclaimed.'

[2] Zuurmond, *Novum Testamentum aethiopice: The Synoptic Gospels*. Part I, 129.

[3] For these dates, cf. Uhlig, *Äthiopische Paläographie*, 105–07, 137–40.

older manuscripts we already have to do with texts that have been revised. Despite this, it does still seem to me possible to say some things about the original translation into Geez and its *Vorlage*.

IV

The fact that the Ethiopic version of the Old Testament follows the Septuagint and its word order very closely and the existence within the Ethiopic of transliterations from the Greek, and of mistakes that can only be explained in terms of the Greek, point conclusively to the view that the Ethiopic version was made primarily, if not necessarily exclusively, from a Greek text; the evidence is too well established to need exemplification here.[1] It seems, however, unlikely that a single recension or a single text-type was used as the basis of the translation of the entire Old Testament, as is indicated already by the variety of suggestions about the underlying Greek text that have been made. We have already noted the view that the translation was made from the Lucianic recension, but although this may be true in one or two individual cases, as a generalisation this is quite improbable.[2] The view of Charles that the translators used the Hexapla also seems quite unlikely.[3] Fuhs has suggested that the Greek *Vorlage* of the Ethiopic

---

[1] Examples of all three types of evidence are to be found in chapters 2 and 3 below; cf. Löfgren, *Daniel*, XLVII–XLVIII.

[2] See above, p. 15, n. 4.

[3] R. H. Charles, 'Ethiopic Version', Hasting's *Dictionary of the Bible* I (1898), 792. The idea that a copy of the Hexapla would have been available in the Aksumite kingdom strains credulity, but even apart from this Charles's argument seems flawed. Charles suggests that certain divergencies of the Ethiopic from the Septuagint can be explained from Symmachus and Aquila, and that it is therefore reasonable to conclude that the Hexapla was used by the translators; he quotes Lam. 2:13, 3:44 and 5:13 (so apparently read for 5:15) as examples of dependence on Symmachus, but admits that the last two examples could be explained from the Hebrew. In fact Charles appears to have relied on

version of Hosea and Micah was of Hesychian origin,[1] but this does not seem very helpful in view of the doubts that exist as to the possibility of identifying this supposed recension.[2]

Of much greater utility have been the suggestions linking the Ethiopic with specific manuscripts and text-types, but here also there has been a very considerable variety of view. Thus Rahlfs, supported by Gehman and Brock, argued that a text-type related to Vaticanus lay behind a number of Old Testament books,[3] Schäfers maintained that the Ethiopic Jeremiah was based on the text represented by the

---

manuscripts with a revised text. Thus in 2:13 አስተማስለኪ፡ does not agree with Symm. εξισωσω σε against all other witnesses, as Charles suggests. The older manuscripts have በምንት፡ አስተማስለኪ፡ ወለተ፡ ኢየሩሳሌም፡ መኑ፡ ያድኅነኪ፡, which corresponds to τι ομιωσω σοι, θυγατερ Ιερουσαλημ; τις σωσει σε (so SAQ).

[1] Fuhs, *Micha*, 37; id., *Hosea*, 121. Cf. C. H. Cornill, *Das Buch des Propheten Ezechiel*, Leipzig, 1886, 66–71; Löfgren, *Daniel*, L.

[2] Cf. Brock, 'Bibelübersetzungen I.2: Die Übersetzungen des Altes Testaments ins Griechische', *TRE* 6 (1980), 167.

[3] Rahlfs argued for this case in relation to the books of Kingdoms, the Psalter, and the book of Ruth; see *Septuaginta–Studien I–III²*, 95, 100–103, 160; id., *Studie über den griechischen Text des Buches Ruth* (MSU III.2 = Nachrichten von der Königl. Gesellschaft der Wissenschaften zu Göttingen, Phil.-Hist. Klasse, 1922), Göttingen, 1922, 134–35. Cf. H. S. Gehman, *JAOS* 52 (1932), 262–63: 'There is no question that a Greek text similar to that of B is the basis of the Old Ethiopic version of Ecclesiastes'; Brock, *TRE* 6 (1980), 206: 'Für die meisten Bücher wurde sie [the Ethiopic translation] aus einem griechischen Texttyp angefertigt, der eng verwandt mit B und relative frei von hexaplarischem Einfluss ist.' See also Knibb, 'The Ethiopic Translation of the Psalms', in A. Aejmelaeus and U. Quast (eds), *Der Septuaginta-Psalter und seine Tochterübersetzungen. Symposium in Göttingen 1997* (MSU XXIV), Göttingen [forthcoming], where it is argued that although the Ethiopic translation of the Psalter belongs with the B-text, it was influenced by a manuscript belonging to the A-text such as 55 or 1219.

original hand in Sinaiticus,[1] and Cornill that the Ethiopic Ezekiel was based on a text-type related to Alexandrinus.[2] More recently Löfgren and Fuhs have attempted to link the Ethiopic texts of Daniel, of Micah and of Hosea to specific miniscules; their results in part overlap, as we should expect for a group of related prophetic texts.[3] The implication of all this, if it may be assumed that the evidence has been interpreted correctly, is that individual books were based on different textual types. This should not, however, surprise us; the translators will have used whatever Greek texts were to hand, and we cannot assume that they will all have been of the same type. In practice the relationship of the manuscripts used to the two major text-types represented by Vaticanus and Alexandrinus is likely to have varied from book to book. It does appear, however, that the Ethiopic version is largely, but not entirely, free of Hexaplaric additions.[4]

If what has been said so far seems relatively clear, it is much less clear whether more than one Greek text was used for the original

[1] Schäfers, *Die äthiopische Übersetzung des Propheten Jeremias*, 156–70. Ziegler (*Ieremias*[2], 31–33) accepts that Schäfers was essentially correct, but notes that there are many unique readings in S which Eth does not share. Ziegler also notes that Eth often agrees with unique readings in 130, and that this miniscule is closely related to the Ethiopic version of Ezekiel and Daniel; see the following notes.

[2] Cornill, *Ezechiel*, 39, 66–71. Ziegler (*Septuaginta. Vetus Testamentum Graecum Auctoritate Academiae Scientiarum Gottingensis editum*. Vol. XVI,1: *Ezechiel*, 2. Auflage, Göttingen, 1977, 19 (and n.1), 29) lists the Ethiopic as a witness to the A-text, but denies that the relationship was very close. He argues that of the miniscules, 130(–534) is most closely related to the Ethiopic; but there is also a close relationship with 106–410, cf. Knibb, *JSS* 33 (1988), 28–29.

[3] Thus Löfgren (*Daniel*, XLVIII–L) argued for dependence on the type of text represented by the miniscules 26, 89 (=239), 130, and 230, particularly 130, and Fuhs (*Micha*, 35–38; *Hosea*, 120–22) argued in the case of Micah for dependence on a text closely related to 26, 239, and 91, particularly 26, and in the case of Hosea for dependence on a text closely related to 239, 130, 26, and 311, particularly 239 and 26.

[4] Cf. e.g. Ziegler, *Ezechiel*[2], 19; Brock, *TRE* 6 (1980), 206.

translation, or for its revision, and whether use was made for the original translation of texts in other languages, specifically Syriac or Hebrew,[1] in addition to the Greek text which clearly formed its main basis. With regard to the first question, we do not so obviously have the situation in the case of the Old Testament that occurs in the case of the gospels, where readings in different manuscripts or groups of manuscripts of, say, the Gospel of Mark appear to have their origin in different parts of the Greek textual tradition.[2] Nevertheless there is some evidence to suggest that more than one Greek text was used. Thus in the case of Ezekiel, for example, Ziegler identified 130–534 as the miniscules to which the Ethiopic is most closely related, but there is an equal, if not closer relationship with the miniscules 106–410.[3] The agreements with these two different pairs of manuscripts, which belong to different textual types,[4] may point to the use by the translators of more than one Greek text, or possibly to the revision of the translation on the basis of a Greek text different from that used for the original translation. Any such use of Greek texts for the purposes of revision is likely to have been at an early stage and certainly well before the beginning of the seventh century and the decline of the Aksumite kingdom.

V

The question of whether the translators made use in addition of a Syriac or a Hebrew text demands more extensive consideration. The

---

[1] The occasional use of the Coptic version at a later stage to correct the Ethiopic cannot be excluded, but it is widely recognised that the Coptic was not used as the basis of the original translation.

[2] Cf. Zuurmond, *Novum Testamentum aethiopice: The Synoptic Gospels.* Part I, 48–67 (especially 53–56, 59–63), 130–32.

[3] See Knibb, *JSS* 33 (1988), 28–29.

[4] 130–534 belongs to the Catena group, 106–410 to the A-text.

likelihood of the use of a Syriac text is closely linked to the view that the Nine Saints, or other similar groups of missionaries, were responsible for the translation, and that these missionaries were Syrian, and it is desirable to examine first the evidence for these two ideas.

As we have already noted, a majority of scholars would attribute the translation of the Bible into Geez to the Nine Saints, or to other similar groups of monks,[1] and this view is now almost taken for granted.[2] It is important to recognize, however, that this view has only very limited support within Ethiopian tradition. So far as I am aware, the earliest reference to such a view is to be found in the statement by Ludolf that the Jesuits had reported that the Nine Saints translated the scriptures into Ethiopic.[3] Apart from this statement, there is only the tradition in the Gadla Libânos linking Mattâ' and the Gospel of Matthew, on the basis of which Conti Rossini asserted that Mattâ' (Libanos) translated the Gospel of Matthew.[4] But the evidence for this

[1] See above, pp. 14–17 and n. 2 on p. 15.

[2] Cf. e.g. Sergew Hable Sellassie, *Ancient and Medieval Ethiopian History*, 119–20; Munro-Hay, *Aksum: An African Civilisation of Late Antiquity*, 14; id., *Ethiopia and Alexandria*, 76; Brakmann, *Die Einwurzelung der Kirche*, 134. See also B. M. Metzger, *The Early Versions of the New Testament: Their Origin, Transmission, and Limitations*, Oxford, 1977, 221–23.

[3] H. Ludolf, *Commentarius ad suam Historiam Aethiopicam*, Francofurti ad Moenum, 1691, 295: 'Scribunt PP. Societatis in epistolis annuis [de annis 1607 & 1608] quod novem illi Sancti ... Sacram Scripturam ex Arabica in Chaldaicam (i.e. Aethiopicam) linguam transtulerint.' Conti Rossini ('Sulla versione e sulla revisione delle sacre scritture in etiopico', 236–37) used this tradition in support of the view that the Nine Saints were responsible for the translation; but see the critical comments of Rahlfs ('Die äthiopische Bibelübersetzung', *Septuaginta–Studien I–III*[2], 666–68). — A useful summary of Ludolf's own views on the subject of the translation of the Bible is given by Hackspill ('Die äthiopische Evangelienübersetzung', 119–21).

[4] Conti Rossini, *Storia d'Etiopia*, 157: 'Per sette anni dimora in Bacla, ove traduce l'evangelo di Matteo'; cf. pp. 158, 223. See above, p. 15, n. 1.

assertion is not all that strong. Conti Rossini was relying on the
version of the Gadla Libânos that he edited,[1] and the tradition does
not occur in the related Homily on Mattâ', which, as Getatchew Haile
has pointed out, appears to contain a more original version of the
traditions concerning Mattâ'.[2] Furthermore, the Gadla Libânos does
not itself state unambiguously that the saint 'translated' the Gospel of
Matthew, merely that he 'wrote' it:

ወነበረ ፡ በበቀላ ፡ ፯ ፡ ዓመተ ፡ ውስተ ፡ ክርሡ ፡ ፰ላዕት ፡ ወጸሐፈ ፡ በሀየ ፡
ወንጌለ ፡ ማቴዎስ ፡ ብፁዕ ፡ [3]

> And he stayed in Baqla for seven years in a cave and there
> wrote the Gospel of the blessed Matthew.

There is thus no early or well-established tradition associating the
Nine Saints with the translation of the Bible. On the other hand, there
is an explicit tradition in BN Éth. 113 (Zotenberg, No. 113) that the
translation of the Old Testament was made in the time of Solomon:

> Quant aux livres de l'Ancien Testament, ils avaient été traduits
> de l'hébreu en gheez du temps de la reine du Midi, lorsqu'elle
> visita Salomon. Or la traduction des livres des Prophètes se
> trouvant en Abyssinie était fidèle; car (les habitants), avant la
> naissance du Christ, étaient attachés à la religion juive. Mais
> dans la traduction faite après la naissance du Christ, ceux qui
> l'avaient crucifié (les juifs) changèrent le vrai texte en
> témoinage mensonger.[4]

The passage, of which this extract forms a part, is concerned to defend
the purity and reliability of the Ethiopic translation of the Old and

---

[1] Conti Rossini, *Ricordi di un soggiorno in Eritrea*, fasc. I, V–VI, 23–41.

[2] Getatchew Haile, 'The Homily of Abba Eleyas, Bishop of Aksum, on Mätta'', 29–35;
note his comment on p. 34: 'Conti Rossini's assertion, relying on the information
received from the much reworked *gädl* of the saint, that Libanos/Mätta' was the
translator into Ge'ez of the Gospel of Matthew needs a stronger evidence.'

[3] Conti Rossini, *Ricordi di un soggiorno in Eritrea*, fasc. I, 26.

[4] H. Zotenberg, *Catalogue des manuscrits éthiopiens (gheez et amharique) de la
Bibliothèque Nationale*, Paris, 1877, 127; cf. Ullendorff, *Ethiopia and the Bible*, 31–32.

New Testaments, and there is no suggestion that it contains reliable historical information. But it is significant that this passage does not refer to the Nine Saints in connection with the translation of the Bible.[1]

Notwithstanding the above, it remains a possibility that foreign missionaries did play an active role in the translation of the scriptures into Geez, and the question that then arises is whether the widely-held view that the missionaries were Syrian in origin is justified. The case for this view was developed particularly by Guidi[2] and by Conti Rossini[3] and was based on three main arguments; but the force of these arguments has been considerably weakened by the considerations advanced by Polotsky[4] and, more recently, by Marrassini.[5]

Firstly it was argued that the names of the missionaries reproduce Syriac personal names or the names of famous religious centres in Syria, and that the places from which they came lead us back to Syria or to neighbouring regions.[6] Against this, Marrassini has pointed out that of the places of origin given for the Ṣadqan, for Libanos, and for the Nine Saints, only Antioch and Caesarea were of real 'Syriac' provenance, and that these were so well-known, and so

[1] Cf. Rahlfs, 'Die äthiopische Bibelübersetzung', *Septuaginta–Studien I–III*[2], 668.

[2] See Guidi, 'Le traduzioni degli Evangelii in arabo e in etiopico', *MRAL*, ser. iv, vol. 4 (1888), 33–34 and n. 1; cf. id., 'La chiesa abissina' *Oriente Moderno* 2 (1922/23), 126; *Storia della letteratura etiopica*, 13–15.

[3] See Conti Rossini, 'Note per la storia letteraria abissina', *RRAL*, ser. v, vol. 8 (1899), 199–201; cf. id., *Storia d'Etiopia*, 155–56, 161–63, 223–25; 'La leggenda di Abbâ Afsê in Etiopia', 151–52, 155.

[4] Polotsky, 'Aramaic, Syriac, and Geʽez', 1–10.

[5] P. Marrassini, 'Some Considerations on the Problem of the "Syriac Influences" on Aksumite Ethiopia', *JES* 23 (1990), 35–46. Cf. P. Piovanelli, 'Sulla *Vorlage* aramaica dell'Enoch etiopico', *Studi Classici e Orientali* (Pisa) 37 (1987), 552–55.

[6] See particularly Guidi, 'Le traduzioni degli Evangelii in arabo e in etiopico', 33–34, n. 1; Conti Rossini, *Storia d'Etiopia*, 161; 'La leggenda di Abbâ Afsê in Etiopia', 155.

frequently cited, that it must be questioned whether the mention of them is anything more than literary convention.[1] As to the names of the missionaries,[2] Marrassini has shown that although most of them cannot be explained by means of the Ethiopian languages, an explanation through Syriac is no more satisfactory. Thus he suggests that the name Garima (ገሪማ ፡) is Arabian, that Afse (አፍጼ ፡) and Matta' (መጣዕ ፡) are to be explained as Arabic forms, that Yohanni (ዮሐኒ ፡) is Coptic, and that an explanation in Syriac terms (via ܣܒܐ) is unnecessary for the name Aragawi (አረጋዊ ፡ , literally 'the elder') given to Michael, one of the leading figures among the Nine Saints. He further suggests that the explanations in terms of Syriac offered for the names Alef (አሌፍ ፡) and Liqanos (ሊቃኖስ ፡) are merely 'impressionistic', and that only the comparison of Guba (ጉባ ፡) with Bet Guba may be plausible.[3]

Secondly it was argued, particularly by Guidi, that the transcription of proper names into Ethiopic followed the Aramaic rule, ቀ = κ, ኀ = χ, ጠ = τ, ተ = θ.[4] However, Marrassini has demonstrated that these transcriptions cannot be described only as

[1] Marrassini, 'Some Considerations', 35–36.

[2] Guidi and Conti Rossini suggested a comparison with Syriac personal names or the names of religious centres in Syria for the following eight names: Matta', Iohanni, Liqanos, Guba, Alef, Garima, Aragawi, Afse.

[3] Marrassini, 'Some Considerations', 36–38. — The compariosn between Guba and Bet Guba was made by both Guidi and Conti Rossini. With regard to Bet Guba, Dr S. P. Brock has suggested to me that the reference intended was probably to the Monastery of Gubba Barraya, which was a prominent monastery in the sixth and seventh centuires, but whose location is uncertain; for this monastery, see E. Honigmann, *Évêques et Évêchés monophysites d'Asie antérieure au VIe siècle* (CSCO 127, Subs. 2), Leuven, 1951, 205. I am grateful to Dr Brock both for the suggestion of Gubba Barraya and for kindly providing the bibliographical reference.

[4] Guidi, 'Le traduzioni degli Evangelii in arabo e in etiopico', 33–34, n. 1; cf. Conti Rossini, *Storia d'Etiopia*, 156; 'La leggenda di Abbâ Afsê in Etiopia', 151.

Aramaic (Guidi) or Syriac (so Conti Rossini), but that every Semitic language transcribes the Greek sounds in this way.[1]

Finally it was argued that the occurrence of supposedly Christian Aramaic and Syriac loanwords in the Ethiopic translation of the Bible provided strong evidence for linking the translation with Syriac-speaking missionaries.[2] Thus, to take an example which has been significant in the discussion, Guidi drew attention to the word ሃይማኖት ፡ , 'faith'; he maintained that the use of ܗܝܡܢܘܬܐ in the sense of πίστις, 'faith', that is, the Christian faith, was peculiar to Syriac from the New Testament onwards, and that this was a clear indication that those· who introduced the word into Geez were Syrians.[3] However, in an important study Polotsky showed that the majority of the loanwords to which appeal was made were borrowed from Jewish Aramaic, not Syriac, and belonged to the pre-Christian Jewish element in Ethiopian Christianity.[4] Subsequent studies have only

---

[1] Marrassini, 'Some Considerations', 39–41.

[2] See particularly Conti Rossini, *Storia d'Etiopia*, 155. Conti Rossini listed nineteen Ethiopic words pertaining to the church or the liturgy that were supposedly of Syriac origin, and a further sixteen words with commercial connotations; he recognised that some of these words could be of Jewish origin, but argued that the Syriac origin of twelve of these (eight terms pertaining to religion and four to commerce) was certain. Cf. earlier J. Gildemeister, Letter to C. R. Gregory of 20 April 1882, printed in Gregory, *Novum Testamentum Graece* (ed. C. Tischendorf), 8th edn, vol. 3: *Prolegomena*, 1894, 895–97; F. Prätorius, *Aethiopische Grammatik*, Berlin, 1886 (reprinted New York, 1955), 3; id., 'Äthiopische Bibelübersetzungen' *RE*[3] 3 (1897), 89; Littmann, 'Geschichte des äthiopische Litteratur', 194, 223–24, especially 224. — For the whole question of loanwords in Ethiopic, see T. Nöldeke, 'Lehnwörter in und aus dem Äthiopischen', *Neue Beiträge zur semitischen Sprachwissenschaft*, Strassburg, 1910, 31–66.

[3] Guidi, *Storia della letteratura etiopica*, 14.

[4] Polotsky, 'Aramaic, Syriac, and Ge'ez', 1–10, especially 3–7, 10. Thus with regard to ሃይማኖት ፡ , Polotsky, although not claiming certainty, argued that its use in the Ethiopic Bible was actually easier to understand if it was borrowed in the first instance as a Jewish

served to reinforce this conclusion. Edward Ullendorff examined thirty-five loanwords in Ethiopic and argued that of these, fifteen were clearly of Jewish Aramaic origin, sixteen were dialectically neutral, and only four (ሐናፈ ፡ ('pagan'), ቀሲስ ፡ ('priest'), ተጸልበ ፡ ('to crucify'), ቍርባን ፡ ('sacrifice, eucharist')) were characteristically Syriac and distinctively Christian in meaning. He attributed these four to a later linguistic layer than the Jewish Aramaic borrowings and suggested that the evidence justified the assumption of two independent strands of Aramaic loanwords in Ethiopic originating from different Aramaic dialects and different periods.[1] However, of the four Syriac loanwords identified by Ullendorff, it is probably only ቀሲስ ፡ that can be said to be clearly Syriac in origin.

In his more recent study Marrassini has attempted to bring some precision into the discussion by taking account both of the results of previous discussions and of evidence culled from Leslau's *Comparative Dictionary of Ge'ez*. He argues that there are no more than six words connected with religious activity for which a Syriac provenance is evident: ዕልዌ ፡ /ዐልዌ ፡ ('aloe', cf. ܥܠܘܝ); ቀሲስ ፡ (cf. ܩܫܝܫܐ); ተፈስስ ፡ ('to draw by lot', cf. ܦܣܐ); ብርያሚን ፡ ('Books of Chronicles', cf. Syr. beryâmîn[2]); ዛዌት ፡ ('Psalter', cf. ܙܡܪ); ሊቅር ፡ ('belt of priests', cf. ܩܡܪܐ).[3] His conclusion that a total of five or six words with clear religious connotations provides weak evidence for positing Syriac influence seems fully justified.[4]

---

word. Cf. Rahlfs, 'Die äthiopische Bibelübersetzung', *Septuaginta–Studien I–III*[2], 674–75.

[1] Ullendorff, *Ethiopia and the Bible*, 119–25, cf. 39–40, n. 6.

[2] Properly ܒܪܝܡܝܢ, from דברי הימים. The Ethiopic forms ብርያሚን ፡ and ድርያሚን ፡ are both corruptions of ድብርያሚን ፡ ; cf. A. Dillmann, *Lexicon linguae aethiopicae*, Leipzig, 1865 (reprinted, New York, 1955), col. 1096.

[3] Marrassini, 'Some Considerations', 38–39. Marrassini notes that the last of these words is attested only in medieval Geez and is possibly a late loanword.

[4] Marrassini notes that it would be possible to add from Leslau's *Dictionary* about fifteen words with secular connotations, but that this provides evidence only of a general

Overall it may be argued that the case for the alleged involvement of Syriac-speaking missionaries in the translation of the Bible into Ethiopic is not proven. Marrassini overstates the case when he concludes that the people who translated the Bible into their own language must have been the Ethiopians themselves,[1] but what is clear is that the arguments used in the past provide no justification for the assumption that the translators must have been Syrian. The use of Greek for the coinage and for royal inscriptions[2] shows that there were those at the Aksumite court who had a knowledge of Greek,[3] and it would be natural to look for the translators in such circles. It remains the case that there could have been influence on the translation from Syriac sources,[4] or even that Syriac-speakers could have been actively involved in the translation; but this has to be demonstrated from the Ethiopic translation itself in the context of the fact that the translation was clearly made, at least primarily, from a Greek text.

In the light of the above, I would like to revert to the question of whether there is evidence for the use by those who translated the Old Testament into Ethiopic of a Syriac text in addition to a Greek text. At first sight there does appear to be such evidence in that there are numerous instances of agreement between the Ethiopic and Syriac versions of the Old Testament. The evidence is syntactical, lexical and

---

cultural influence from Syria, not of influence specifically in the religious sphere. Witakowski ('Syriac Influences in Ethiopian Culture', 192) has in fact argued that some other words besides those listed by earlier scholars 'may turn out to be of Syriac origin', and he suggests some examples; but the point made by Marrassini remains relevant.

[1] Marrassini, 'Some Considerations', 41–42.

[2] For royal inscriptions in Greek (RIÉth 269–71, 275, 277, 286), see Bernand, Drewes, Schneider, Anfray, *Recueil des inscriptions de l'Éthiopie*, tome I, 359–87; tome II, planches 178–82.

[3] Cf. Munro-Hay, *Aksum: An African Civilisation of Late Antiquity*, 149, 245–47.

[4] Cf. Marrassini, 'Some Considerations', 42.

textual and may be illustrated by reference to the translation of Ezekiel.

Examples of agreement between the Ethiopic and the Syriac in the syntactical sphere are the frequent common use of imperatives — particularly in commands to the prophet to address the people — where the Greek has the future tense corresponding to *waw* consecutive with the perfect in Hebrew (e.g. 13:18; 14:4); or the frequent common use of perfect or imperfect forms where the Greek has τοῦ plus the infinitive corresponding to Hebrew ל with the infinitive construct (e.g. 16:26; 17:15, 18); or the use of 'that' and 'that not' (ከመ : and ከመ : ኢ in Ethiopic, ד and ܕܠܐ in Syriac) after the oath formula 'As I live, says the Lord' in place of the Greek and Hebrew 'if not' and 'if' (e.g. 14:16; 20:3; 33:11).

In the sphere of vocabulary there are a number of Greek words for which the Ethiopic and the Syriac versions use the same, or a similar, rendering. For example, the formula 'I will stretch out (Greek ἐκτείνειν, Hebrew נטה) my hand against' regularly becomes 'I will raise (Ethiopic አንሥአ : , Syriac ܐܪܝܡ) my hand against' (e.g. 14:9, 13; 16:27). The use of እለ : ተርፉ : (literally 'those who are left') as the standard equivalent for Greek οἱ καταλοίποι ('the remnant') has in three instances (5:10; 9:8; 17:21) an exact counterpart in the Syriac use of the Eshtaph'al of ܐܪ with ܕ. Thus in 5:10, for example, the Ethiopic renders πάντας τοὺς καταλοίπους σου (MT את כל שאריתך) by ኵሎ : ተርፈ : ውስቴትከ : (literally 'those who are left among you'). This corresponds to the Syriac ܐܪܠܝܢ ܕܐܫܬܚܪܬ ܒܟܘܢ not only in the expression used, but also in the omission of πάντας. The rendering of ἰδού ('behold') in Ethiopic by ረከብኩ : (literally 'I found', and hence 'I saw, I perceived') is commonplace and occurs seven times in Ezekiel. In one of these (8:8) it has an exact counterpart in the Syriac in the use of ܐܫܟܚܬ, and in four other passages (8:7, 14; 11:1; 40:3) the Syriac may provide the general background for the use of ζⁿⁿⁱⁱ፦ inasmuch as it uses ܚ ܠܘ ('I saw') for ἰδού.[1]

The rendering of ἐχόμενος, the middle participle of ἔχειν ('to have, hold') used with the meaning 'next to, following' is particularly instructive. The closest equivalent in Ethiopic is ኅትዝ፦, the participle of the corresponding verb ኅገዝ፦, and this is actually used for ἐχόμενος in 1:9. It is also used in 10:16a where the Greek ἐχόμενοι αὐτῶν is rendered in Ethiopic by ኅትዝን፦ ምስሊሆሙ፦ (a double translation, literally 'near with them'[2]) and in Syriac by ܥܡܗܘܢ ('with them'). The majority of the remaining occurrences of ἐχόμενος in Ezekiel are rendered either by ምስለ፦ ('with', so 1:19; 3:13; 10:19; 11:22), where the Syriac always has ܥܡ ('with'), or by ኀበ፦ ('at, near, by the side of', so 9:2; 10:6, 9a; 42:1bis; 48:21), where the Syriac has either ܥܠ ܝܕ ('near') or ܠܩܘܒܠ ('opposite to, over against'). Thus the choice of the word used for ἐχόμενος in the Ethiopic corresponds to what is used in the Syriac.[3]

The treatment of ἐχόμενος is linked to a tendency that is sometimes observable for the Ethiopic to use a word with a more precise meaning than the underlying Greek word. In some of these cases the Ethiopic corresponds to the Syriac, as, for example, in some of the renderings of the very common word διδόναι ('to give, to set', Hebrew נתן). Thus in 18:8 and 13 διδόναι is used with reference to lending at interest, where both the Ethiopic and the Syriac use a verb meaning 'to lend' (ለቅሕ፦, ܐܘܙܦ). In 25:4 διδόναι is used of pitching a tent, where Ethiopic and Syriac use a verb with the meaning 'to pitch' (ተክለ፦, ܢܩܫ). And in 27:14, 18 and 22 διδόναι is used of

---

[1] The other two references are 3:23; 8:4.

[2] Similarly in 10:16b ምስሊሆሙ፦ ኅትዝን፦ occurs for απο των εχομενα αυτων; but the Syriac has only ܥܡܗܘܢ.

[3] There are three other occurrences of ἐχόμενος in Ezekiel. In two of these Eth uses respectively ለ (10:9b) and ቅሩብ፦ (48:13) as alternatives for ኀበ፦; in 1:15 Eth ታሕተ፦ ('under') perhaps reflects the influence of 1:8.

supplying goods to a market, where Ethiopic and Syriac both use a verb meaning 'to bring' (አምጽአ ፡ , ܐܝܬܝ).

There are also a fair number of textual agreements between the Ethiopic and the Syriac, many of which involve the omission or insertion of individual words and phrases or the simplification of the text. Two striking examples may be mentioned here. In 1:9 the Ethiopic has a simplified version of the underlying text and reads 'and when they (the living creatures) moved, they moved straight forward and did not turn'. This simplified version corresponds to the Syriac and clearly does not follow the Greek or the Hebrew:

ወሶበ ፡ የሐውሩ ፡ ርቱዐ ፡ የሐውሩ ፡ ወኢይትመየጡ ፡

ܘܟܕ ܐܙ̈ܠܝܢ ܩܕܡܝܗܘܢ ܐܝ̈ܠ ܗܘܘ, ܘܠܐ ܡܬܦܢܝܢ ܗܘܘ.

οὐκ ἐπεστρέφοντο ἐν τῷ βαδίζειν αὐτά, ἕκαστον
κατέναντι τοῦ προσώπου αὐτῶν ἐπορεύοντο

לֹא יִסַּבּוּ בְּלֶכְתָּן אִישׁ אֶל־עֵבֶר פָּנָיו יֵלֵכוּ

In 39:20, in the Gog section, the Greek and Hebrew have 'and you will be filled at my table with horses', but the Ethiopic and the Syriac read 'with the flesh of horses' — the same reading that occurs in the Targum.

The examples that have been discussed above vary in their significance, but the evidence as a whole makes it clear that there was influence of some kind from the Syriac version on the Ethiopic version of Ezekiel. This finding in respect of Ezekiel may be compared with that of Fuhs who identified a number of passages in Micah and Hosea where the Old Ethiopic — the closest it is possible to get to the original translation — had been influenced by the Syriac. But the problem is that we cannot be certain that this Syriac influence is to be attributed to the time of the original translation of the Old Testament into Ethiopic in the fifth or sixth century. On the contrary, it has often been assumed that Syriac influence on the Ethiopic version was mediated through Arabic sources and belongs essentially to the revision of the text that occurred in the fourteenth century. Fuhs himself speaks in terms of a Syro-Arabic influence on the Old Ethiopic, and although he allows for the possibility that this influence was exerted prior to the fourteenth century, he clearly does not envisage that the translators themselves were directly influenced by the Syriac.[1] Earlier this century Schäfers demonstrated in relation to Jeremiah that one layer of the Ethiopic textual tradition, the so-called vulgar recension, had been strongly influenced by an Arabic text that was closely related to the Syriac version.[2] But so far as the Old Ethiopic was concerned, he argued that apparent instances of Syriac influence were to be attributed to infection from the Syro-Arabic source rather than to direct influence from the Syriac itself.[3] And the situation in respect of Ezekiel is entirely in accordance with this view.

The Arabic version of Ezekiel exists in two main forms, one based on a Greek text similar to that in Alexandrinus, the other based on a Syriac text.[4] The former type of text is the one that was included in Walton's Polyglott and is represented, for example, in one of the Arabic manuscripts in the British Library (BL Orient. 1326). It is not clear whether this type of text had any influence on the Ethiopic text of Ezekiel, but if so, it was very limited. The Syriac-based type of text is represented, for example, in an Arabic manuscript of the Prophets

[1] Cf. Fuhs, *Micha*, 35: 'An einigen Stellen weist aber der Text offensichtlich syrisch-arabische Einflüsse auf, die schon sehr früh in den Text eingedrungen sein müssen; jedenfalls noch vor der Ende des 14.Jh. einsetzenden syrisch-arabischen Rezension'; id., *Hosea*, 114–15.

[2] Schäfers, *Die äthiopische Übersetzung des Propheten Jeremias*, VII, 1–26.

[3] Cf. Schäfers, *Die äthiopische Übersetzung des Propheten Jeremias*, 155: 'Von [Arab. (Syr.)] aber wissen wir, dass seine Lesarten mit dem Altäth. in der "vulgaren" äthiopischen Bibelrezension in weitesten Umfange verbunden worden sind. Von hier aus war natürlich der Weg leicht und nahe, auf dem eine Infektion des unrezensierten Altäthiopen mit Lesarten von Arab. (Syr.) vor sich gehen konnte. Diesen Hergang halte ich für warscheinlicher als eine unmittelbar vom Syr. her erfolgte Einwirkung auf den Altäthiopien.'

[4] For the Arabic version of the prophetic books, see G. Graf, *Geschichte der christlichen arabischen Literatur*. Band I: *Die Übersetzungen* (Studi e Testi 118), Città del Vaticano, 1944, 131–37.

in the Bodleian Library (MS. Arch Seld. A. 67), and there is no doubt that in many instances — certainly the majority of the ones discussed above — its readings agree with those of the Ethiopic version. Thus the Syro-Arabic text uses imperatives in place of the Greek future tenses, perfect and imperfect forms in place of τοῦ plus the infinitive, 'that' (Arabic أَنْ) in place of the Greek, and ultimately Hebrew, idiom 'if' after the oath formula (e.g. 14:16; 20:3). In the sphere of vocabulary, the Syro-Arabic text uses the verb رفع ('to raise') in the formula 'I will stretch out my hand against' (e.g. 14:13; 16:27), a relative clause with the verb بَقِى ('to remain') as the equivalent of οἱ καταλοίποι (e.g. 9:8; 17:21), the verb وجد ('to find') in Ezek. 8:8 for ἰδού, and elsewhere the verb رأى ('to see') for ἰδού (e.g. 8:14; 11:1). For ἐχόμενος the Syro-Arabic has مع ('with') in Ezek. 1:19; 3:13; 10:19; 11:22, على جانب ('beside') in 9:2; 10:6, 9bis, and حذاء ('opposite') in 42:1bis; 48:13, 21. In place of διδόναι, the Syro-Arabic text uses قرض (IV) ('to lend') in Ezek. 18:13, ضرب (with the meaning 'to pitch') in Ezek. 25:4, and either أتى ب or أتى (IV) ('to bring') in Ezek. 27:14, 18 and 22. There is likewise agreement between the Syro-Arabic version and the Ethiopic in the textual sphere. In 39:20 the Syro-Arabic has 'with the flesh of horses' (لحوم الخيل), just as in the Syriac and Ethiopic, and in 1:9 it has the same abbreviated text that occurs in the Syriac and Ethiopic: 'and when they moved, they moved straight forward (literally 'in front of them') and did not turn' (وإذا ذهبن يذهبن حذاهن ولا يلتفتن).

The agreements between the Syro-Arabic text and the Ethiopic in the case of Ezekiel, of which the above are only examples,[1] are striking and confirm the view that Syriac influence on the Ethiopic Old Testament was mediated through the Arabic version in the medieval period, a time when we know that Ethiopic literature was heavily influenced by Arabic literature. It remains of course possible

---

[1] However, it is not suggested that it was precisely the text contained in Bodleian MS. Arch Seld. A. 67 that served as the *Vorlage* for the revision of the Ethiopic text of Ezekiel.

that there was also some Syriac influence on the Ethiopic version at the time of the original translation. But there is no unambiguous textual evidence to support this, and very strong evidence — in the Syro-Arabic version — which suggests otherwise.

VI

In recent years Edward Ullendorff, both in his Schweich Lectures and in other publications, has been the person who has most forcefully argued for the view that the original translators used not only a Greek and a Syriac text, but also a Hebrew text.[1] In his Schweich Lectures he discussed the general evidence for this view and suggested that there was nothing that had so far come to his notice that 'would prevent us from assuming that all three [Greek, Syriac, and Hebrew] might have been employed, in one form or another, directly or indirectly, by a team of translators.'[2] And in his most recent publication on this subject, which was written in 1981 but only published in 1987, he examined sixty words, mostly taken from Appendix II of Dillmann's Lexicon, the *Index vocabulorum peregrinorum*, that occur in the Ethiopic Old Testament and are, almost without exception, manifestly transliterations directly from the Hebrew. He argued that the introduction of these transliterated Hebrew words into the Ethiopic Old Testament can only plausibly be

---

[1] See the publications listed above, p. 2, n. 1. For direct use of the Hebrew by the original translators, cf. also Charles, 'Ethiopic Version', 792; Heider, *Die aethiopische Bibelübersetzung*, 5, 16–17; but on the latter, see the comments of Schäfers (*Die äthiopische Übersetzung des Propheten Jeremias*, VIII, 178).

[2] Ullendorff, *Ethiopia and the Bible*, 56; cf. id., 'Hebrew, Aramaic and Greek', 257 (= *Studia Aethiopica et Semitica*, 51).

placed in the period of the original translation into Ethiopic, that is in the fourth and fifth centuries.[1]

These transliterated words form an integral part of what is commonly perceived as a thorough-going revision of the Ethiopic text on the basis of the Hebrew, that is the so-called academic recension. They are certainly of considerable interest. It is worth noting that thirty-one of the sixty words come from the book of Ezekiel, the majority from chapters 40–48, and there are in fact many more transliterations from the Hebrew in the later Ethiopic manuscripts of the book than are discussed by Ullendorff.[2] The existence of the transliterations provides clear evidence that those who introduced them into the Ethiopic version of Ezekiel had direct knowledge of the Hebrew text. But the inclusion of the transliterations has often produced a text that is unintelligible in Ethiopic, and it is clear that those responsible had only a limited knowledge of Hebrew. It is difficult to know why so many transliterations were included, but their inclusion suggests a particular regard for the authority of the Hebrew text, and there may have been a wish to produce a complete text corresponding to the Hebrew even, at times, at the cost of intelligibility. Be that as it may, I do not believe that these

[1] Ullendorff, 'Hebrew Elements in the Ethiopic Old Testament', 42–50, cf. p. 50: 'While I am pretty certain, in conclusion, that only during the period of the original Ethiopic Bible translations would the general circumstances have been propitious to generating the Hebrew admixtures which form the substance of this paper, I remain puzled as to the rationale of their creation and acceptance by the Ethiopic Old Testament — except in the very few cases where they were misunderstood as proper names, either by way of the Septuagint or, more usually, without its interposition. A good deal of further thought may need to be given to produce a satisfactory explanation for the existence in the Ethiopic Old Testament of these curious Hebraisms.'

[2] Cf. Knibb, 'The Ethiopic Text of Ezekiel and the Excerpts in *GEBRÄ ḤEMAMAT*', *JSS* 34 (1989),455–56, where some examples in Ezek. 47:2–9a are discussed; but transliterations can be found in the later manuscripts throughout the book of Ezekiel, and particularly in chapters 40–48.

transliterations provide evidence that the original translators had access to and made use of a Hebrew as well as of a Greek text.

So far as Ezekiel is concerned, the most compelling argument against such a view is that these transliterations only occur in manuscripts that date from the sixteenth century or later. They are to be found on the one hand in Cambridge Add. 1570, which contains a unique type of text and is dated to 1588/89,[1] and on the other in manuscripts that contain the academic recension, of which the two most important and oldest representatives are Abbadianus 35 and British Library Add. 24,991, both dating from the seventeenth century. It is obviously not the case that the date of a manuscript and the date of the text-recension it contains are necessarily the same, and a text with an early form can reappear in a late manuscript. But the complete absence of the transliterated Hebrew words from the older manuscripts is very difficult to explain if the transliterations — and the use of Hebrew texts — do go back to the time of the original translation. Thus in view of the date of the manuscripts containing the transliterations it seems to me difficult to carry back the time of the Hebraising recension of which they form a part to much, if at all, before the sixteenth century.

In greater detail it is to be observed that the thirty-one transliterated words in Ezekiel that Edward Ullendorff examined can be divided into two groups. More than half of them occur in chapters 42–48 in sections of the book of Ezekiel that do not exist in the older Ethiopic manuscripts and appear to have dropped out of the archetype of all the older manuscripts at an early stage — if, that is, they ever formed part of the original translation of the book. In the case of the remaining words, the older manuscripts do not contain these Hebrew readings but rather have a text corresponding to the Greek. Thus, for example, in Ezek. 41:15 the younger manuscripts certainly reproduce the obscure Hebrew word אַתּוּקִיה as ኣቴዌቴ፡ , but the older

---

[1] See E. Ullendorff and S. G. Wright, *Catalogue of Ethiopian Manuscripts in the Cambridge University Library*, Cambridge, 1961, 1–3.

manuscripts have አጸለፈ ፡ , a transliteration of the Greek reading τὰ ἀπόλοιπα, perhaps understood as 'the open spaces'. There are also cases where, although all the Ethiopic manuscripts have a transliterated Hebrew word, there are significant differences in the form of the word as it occurs in the older and younger manuscripts which make it clear that in the former case the transliteration has entered the Ethiopic via the Greek, in the latter directly from the Hebrew. Thus — to take a word not discussed by Edward Ullendorff — the Greek αιλαμ is properly a transliteration of the Hebrew אילם, אולם ('vestibule'), a word used repeatedly in Ezekiel 40–46. But αιλαμ in the Greek Ezekiel also serves as an equivalent for Hebrew איל ('pilaster, pillar') and even of סף ('threshold'). In Ezek. 40:16, by way of example, αιλαμ is used in the Greek three times, and in each case it is reproduced in the older Ethiopic manuscripts as ኤላም ፡ . But in the younger Ethiopic manuscripts there are three different forms, which reproduce the three forms that occur in the Hebrew text: ኤሊሒም ፡ , Hebrew אליהמה ('their pillars'); ኤላሙት ፡ , Hebrew אלמות ('the vestibules'); and ኤል ፡ or ኤላ ፡ , Hebrew איל ('the pillar'). There is little doubt that in this and many similar cases it is only the younger Ethiopic manuscripts that show direct dependence on the Hebrew, and that in the older manuscripts the transliteration came into the text from the Greek.

The situation that I have just described for the transliterations in Ezekiel is repeated in the case of other books,[1] and the view that the transliterations from the Hebrew do not go back to the time of the original translation is reinforced by other considerations concerning the date of the academic recension and of possible influence from the Hebrew. Thus Schäfers pointed out that no manuscript representative

---

[1] In Dan. 11:30, for example, ጺም ፡ ወከቲም ፡ ወነካህ ፡ is clearly based on (a misreading of) the Hebrew ציים כתים ונכאה, as Ullendorff observes ('Hebrew, Aramaic and Greek', 254 (= *Studia Aethiopica et Semitica*, 48)); but the Ethiopic reading is found only in the later manuscripts, whereas the older manuscripts either do not have the passage or provide a translation based on a Syro-Arabic text.

of the academic recension was copied before 1600.[1] Schäfers no doubt had in mind in the first instance the manuscripts of Jeremiah that he assigned to the academic recension, namely Bodleian MS. Bruce 75 (Dillmann, no. VI) and Berlin Ms. orient. quart. 986,[2] but the same is true of other manuscripts that have been assigned to this recension, such as Abbadianus 35, BL Add. 24,991, BL Orient. 496, BL Orient. 498, which all date from the seventeenth century.[3] It is, furthermore, difficult to find clear evidence of influence from the Hebrew in manuscripts that are older than this. In his edition of Daniel, Löfgren, who assigned the academic recension to the second half of the fifteenth century or the first half of the sixteenth,[4] noted that there were a significant number of readings in Abbadianus 55, which he dated to about 1500,[5] that agreed with readings in the manuscripts belonging to the academic recension (Abbadianus 35, BL Add. 24,991); he argued that the majority of these readings resulted from the correction of the *Vorlage* of Abbadianus 55, and that the text represented by Abbadianus 35 and BL Add. 24,991 must therefore have separated from the older text by the middle of the fifteenth century at the latest. However, Löfgren also observed that it was not certain whether the revision of the text at that time was based on the

---

[1] Schäfers, *Die äthiopische Übersetzung des Propheten Jeremias*, 155–56.

[2] The section of the Oxford manuscript containing Jeremiah was copied for James Bruce and dates from the eighteenth century, while the Berlin manuscript dates from the seventeenth or eighteenth century; cf. Dillmann, *Catalogus Codicum Manuscriptorum Bibliothecae Bodleianae Oxoniensis. Pars VII: Codices Aethiopici*, Oxford, 1848, 8–9; E. Hammerschmidt and V. Six, *Äthiopische Handschriften 1: Die Handschriften der Staatsbibliothek Preussischer Kulturbesitz* (VOHD XX/4), Wiesbaden, 1983, 200–204.

[3] For the assignment of these manuscripts to the academic recension, cf. e.g. Löfgren, *Daniel*, XLV–XLVII; Fuhs, *Micha*, 33–34. For the dates of these manuscripts, see Conti Rossini, 'Notice', *JA* x.20 (1912), 9–10; Wright, *Catalogue*, 12–14, 18–19.

[4] Löfgren, *Daniel*, XLVII; Fuhs (*Micha*, 34; *Hosea*, 110–11) suggests the same date.

[5] See Löfgren, *Daniel*, XXVII; cf. Conti Rossini, 'Notice', *JA* x.20 (1912), 10–11 (15th or 16th century).

massoretic text, and that only a few passages seemed to suggest this.[1]
But of the three passages to which he pointed (Dan. 9:4, 16; 7:13), it
is only the last where influence from the Hebrew seems a real
possibility.[2] Be that as it may, influence from the Hebrew cannot be
traced in manuscripts that are older than Abbadianus 55, that is, in
manuscripts that date from about 1500 at the earliest. I conclude that
there is no convincing evidence that the Hebrew elements in the
Ethiopic Old Testament go back to the time of the original translation.

VII

I have been primarily concerned in this lecture with the origin of the
translation of the Old Testament into Geez. I will have more to say
about the character of the translation in the remaining two lectures,
but I would like in the final part of this lecture to say a little more
about the history of the text.

In his edition of the Ethiopic Daniel, Löfgren suggested that his
base manuscript — BN Éth. 11 (Zotenberg, no. 7) — was a valuable

---

[1] Löfgren, *Daniel*, XLI–XLII, 131, 139–40.

[2] (1) Dan. 9:4: Abb 55, Abb 35 and BL Add. 24,991 read ኪያነ ፡ (= 𝕸 הברית) for ኪያነከ ፡ ,
but the omission of the pronominal suffix in Abb 55 could well be due to chance and
need not reflect the influence of Abb 35 BL Add. 24,991 or of the Hebrew. (2) Dan. 9:16:
ወነስሩ ፡ ሕዝብከ ፡ በስ ፡ (cf. θ' καὶ ὁ λαός σου εἰς ὀνειδισμὸν ἐγένετο ἐν) has been
corrupted in Abb 55 and BL Orient. 501 to ወነብሩ ፡ ሕዝብከ ፡ በስ ፡ ; Abb 35 and BL
Add. 24,991 have ወነብሩ ፡ ሕዝብከ ፡ ለጽዕሰት ፡ ለ (cf. 𝕸 ועמך לחרפה ל). However, ወነብሩ ፡
is an obvious corruption of ወነስሩ ፡ , and it is not necessary to attribute the occurrence of
ወነብሩ ፡ in Abb 55 BL Orient. 501 to the influence of the text found in Abb 35 BL Add.
24,991, which has been corrected at a second stage on the basis of the Hebrew. (3) Dan.
7:13: only here does it seem possible that the occurrence of ዐቢይ ፡ (Abb 55 መጽአ ፡ ዐቢይ ፡
ደመና ፡ ሰማይ ፡ , Abb 35 BL Add. 24,991 መጽአ ፡ ዐቢይ ፡ በደመና ፡ ሰማይ ፡) reflects the
influence of a misreading of כבר; cf. Ullendorff, 'Hebrew, Aramaic and Greek', 256 (=
Studia Aethiopica et Semitica, 50).

witness to the biblical text as it existed about 1300 in a form that had probably not yet been revised. He also suggested that all the extant manuscripts derived from a common *Vorlage* which gave us access to the Daniel text at about the end of the Zagwe period, that is about the middle of the thirteenth century, but that we could not go back further than this.[1] In view of the age of the Paris manuscript, Löfgren's expectations are probably justified in regard to the text of Daniel. But because we have so few Ethiopic Old Testament manuscripts from before 1350, it seems to me likely that for a significant part of the Old Testament we shall have to be content with the text as it existed in the period of literary revival that occurred in the mid-fourteenth century after the 'restoration' of the Solomonic dynasty, and not the text as it existed in the Zagwe period. To put this another way, it seems to me doubtful whether it is possible across the entire Old Testament to distinguish clearly between what is known as the Old Ethiopic, that is the notionally unrevised text, and the revised text of the fourteenth century, the so-called vulgar recension to which the great majority of the older Ethiopic manuscripts belong. And I suspect that some of the manuscripts that have been regarded as representative of the Old Ethiopic, the unrevised text, do not really merit this attribution.

The type of text that has come to be known as the vulgar recension is contained primarily in the manuscripts of the fifteenth and sixteenth centuries and derives from a process of revision whose origins, as we have noted, can be placed in the fourteenth century in the literary revival that began during the reign of Amda Sion (1314– 1344). It must, however, be doubted whether the term 'recension' is appropriate in this case. There is certainly not the uniformity of text-type that is characteristic of manuscripts from the seventeenth century onwards. Numerous small changes can be observed amongst the manuscripts of the vulgar recension, but they are for the most part the kind of changes that are brought about spontaneously when manuscripts are copied and are not textually based. One obvious

[1] Löfgren, *Daniel*, XLVII–XLVIII.

underlying reason for the changes seems to have been the desire to provide a smoother and more readable text. The manuscripts that represent this text can fairly readily be divided up into separate families, but there has been a considerable degree of cross-infection, and in my experience no one family can consistently be said to have the priority.

Inasmuch as revision in the fourteenth century was textually based, there is little doubt that Arabic texts were used. The Ethiopic Synaxarium records of Abba Salama 'the translator', who held office as archbishop in the latter part of the fourteenth century, that he translated the scriptures from Arabic into Geez,[1] and it is also recorded of him that he was responsible for the translation from Arabic into Geez of numerous hagiographical and patristic texts.[2] In the case of the scriptures, it is clear that they were not translated from Arabic, but rather revised on the basis of Arabic texts, as we have seen, and it has become customary to interpret the tradition about Abba Salama in this sense.[3] In practice, however, the extent to which Arabic texts were used for the revison of the Ethiopic text is likely to have varied considerably from book to book.

The third main stage in the history of the Ethiopic Old Testament is constituted by the Hebraising kind of text that has come to be known as the academic recension and is to be found in

[1] See Guidi, *Le Synaxaire éthiopien. III: Mois de Nahasê et de Pâguemên* (PO ix.4), Paris, 1912, 359; cf. Ludolf, *Commentarius*, 295; Zotenberg, *Catalogue*, 263, under 'o'; Ullendorff, *Ethiopia and the Bible*, 32–33.

[2] For Abba Salama 'the translator', see particularly A. van Lantschoot, 'Abbâ Salâmâ, métropolite de'Éthiopie (1348–1388) et son rôle de traducteur', *Atti del Convegno Internazionale di Studi Etiopici (Roma, 2–4 aprile 1959)* (Accademia Nazionale dei Lincei, Problemi attuali di scienza e di cultura, Quaderno N. 48), Rome, 1960, 397–401. Van Lantschoot maintains that Abba Salama held office from 1348 to 1388 (or perhaps to a little before this).

[3] Cf. Conti Rossini, 'Sulla versione e sulla revisione delle sacre scritture in etiopico', 238–40.

manuscripts that date from the seventeenth century onwards. In this case there is no question but that the term recension is appropriate inasmuch as this kind of text has been subjected to systematic revision. Sometimes the changes that were made were neutral in character or were merely intended to produce a smoother Ethiopic text, and not infrequently readings in the academic recension agree with readings in one strand of the older tradition[1] — as Löfgren observed in relation to the text of Daniel in Abbadianus 55, which he dated to about 1500.[2] But where such agreements occur it is very hard to determine whether at that stage use was made of a Hebrew text. In contrast, in the academic recension proper there are numerous readings involving both changes and additions — sometimes substantial — to the older text that clearly betray knowledge of the Hebrew text and were intended to bring the Ethiopic more into line with the Hebrew. The fact that the academic recension, as we have noted, contains many words transliterated directly from Hebrew makes it quite clear that the textual basis of the revison was the Hebrew Bible itself and not merely a text with a Hebraising tendency such as the Syriac version or the Lucianic recension. The transliterations also make improbable Guidi's suggestion that the textual basis was the Arabic translation of Sa'adya Ga'on,[3] as Löfgren rightly observed.[4]

---

[1] In practice the agreements are normally with one strand of the vulgar tradition.

[2] See above, pp. 39–40.

[3] Cf. Conti Rossini, 'Note per la storia letteraria abissina', 208; Littmann, 'Geschichte des äthiopische Litteratur', 225–26; Guidi, *Storia della letteratura etiopica*, 25. — For the translation of Sa'adya, see Graf, *Geschichte der christlichen arabischen Literatur*. Band I, 101–03.

[4] Löfgren, *Daniel*, XLVI; cf. Ullendorff, *Ethiopia and the Bible*, 58. — Similar considerations also apply to the recent suggestion of Fuhs (*Hosea*, 108–11) that the *Vorlage* of the academic recension was an Arabic text that was based on Hexaplaric or Lucianic Greek manuscripts or directly on the Massoretic text.

It is one thing to recognise the existence of this kind of text, and another to place it in a plausible historical context. Knowledge of Hebrew, even at the limited level reflected in this recension, is unlikely to have been widespread in Ethiopia in the medieval and early modern periods, and indeed this is one of the reasons why Edward Ullendorff has been inclined to place these Hebraisms in the Aksumite period, in the fourth to perhaps the seventh century.[1] Despite this, annotations, which are found in a number of manuscripts, that refer to the Hebrew text or give the meaning of Hebrew words indicate that there was some kind of limited knowledge of Hebrew in the later period.[2] The best known of these annotations are the 'text-critical' notes refering to the Hebrew text and the Arabic version that were inserted in the margin of the Paris manuscript of Job and Daniel (BN Éth. 11 (Zotenberg, no. 7)) by a certain Mercurius.[3] According to Zotenberg, Mercurius 'had collated

---

[1] Ullendorff, *Ethiopia and the Bible*, 57; cf. Littmann, 'Geschichte des äthiopische Litteratur', 225.

[2] Cf. the transliterations of Hebrew words in BN Éth. 113 (Zotenberg, no. 113 (*Catalogue*, p. 128; Ullendorff, *Ethiopia and the Bible*, 32)) and BN Éth. 94 (Zotenberg, no. 5 (*Catalogue*, p. 8)). In addition, texts of a commentary on the Octateuch, particularly Abbadianus 156 (Conti Rossini, no. 59), contain a number of references to 'Hebrew' and 'Arabic'; see R. Cowley, *Ethiopian Biblical Interpretation: A Study in Exegetical Tradition and Hermeneutics* (University of Cambridge Oriental Publications 38), Cambridge, 1988, 102–109. Cowley examined the references in Genesis and noted that while the occurrence of a transliterated Hebrew word (በአቦርኬ ፡ , cf. בעבורך) in the comment on Gen. 12:13 showed that at some stage a Hebrew text was consulted, a number of the comments revealed little, if any, contact with the Massoretic text. He concluded that the author of the commentary 'may have used Geez biblical texts with marginalia referring to variant readings, or Geez biblical texts which were believed to have been corrected on the basis of Hebrew or Arabic (but which in reality contained a *Mischtext*).'

[3] See Zotenberg, *Catalogue*, 11; F. M. Esteves Pereira, *Le livre de Job: version éthiopi-*

the Ethiopic text with the Hebrew text and an Arabic version', and whatever this process may have involved, certainly some of the notes — for example the transliteration of שְׁבְלָה (Job 24:24) as ሰብለ ፡ — reveal knowledge of the Hebrew. Unfortunately we have no information as to how this knowledge was acquired. But Ethiopia was not cut off from the outside world during the fifteenth and sixteenth centuries, the period within which the academic recension is most probably to be placed. There were regular contacts with Europe throughout this period.[1] There were communities of Ethiopian monks in Egypt at Qusqwam, Hara Zuwaila in Cairo, and Scete,[2] and there was a long-established Ethiopian community in Jerusalem.[3] There were regular pilgrimages by Ethiopians who journeyed thorugh Egypt to the holy places in Palestine. Knowledge of Hebrew could well have been acquired by monks who travelled to Jerusalem as pilgrims.[4]

Löfgren dated the academic recension of the book of Daniel to the second half of the fifteenth century or the first half of the

---

enne (PO ii.5), Paris, 1907, 569-70; Löfgren, Daniel, XXIV–XXV; Ullendorff, Ethiopia and the Bible, 42–43.

[1] For early contacts between Ethiopia and Christian Europe, see Taddesse Tamrat, Church and State in Ethiopia, 248–67, particularly 256–67.

[2] Cerulli (Etiopi in Palestina: Storia della comunità etiopica di Gerusalemme, vol. II, Rome, 1947, 353–432) provides a valuable collection of documents relating to the organization and activities of the communities in Egypt and Jerualem. For Ethiopian monks in Egypt, see also O. F. A. Meinardus, Christian Egypt: Faith and Life, Cairo, 1970, 427–35.

[3] For the Ethiopian community in Jerusalem in the fifteenth and sixteenth centuries, see Cerulli, Etiopi in Palestina, vol. I, 200–447; vol. II, 1–51; cf. O. Meinardus, 'The Ethiopians in Jerusalem', Zeitschrift für Kirchengeschichte 76 (1965), 116–25, particularly 121–25.

[4] Ullendorff (Ethiopia and the Bible, 43) speculates that Mercurius is to be identified with one of the individuals mentioned in the documents relating to the communities in Egypt (see Cerulli, Etiopi in Palestina, vol. II, 398, 402) and observes that such an individual 'would have had an opportunity of studying Hebrew and Arabic.'

sixteenth.[1] The latter date would seem less likely in that during the first half of the sixteenth century Ethiopia was embroiled in the wars with the muslims under the leadership of Ahmed Grañ and suffered substantial devastation. It seems to me more plausible to think either in terms of the reign of Zar'a Ya'aqob in the mid-fifteenth century, which was a time of literary activity,[2] or in terms of the latter part of the sixteenth century and specifically of the reign of Sarsa Dengel (1563–1597), when there was at least some recovery. It is perhaps not without interest that it was in the reign of Sarsa Dengel that an Old Testament manuscript, now in Cambridge University Library, which has a unique and markedly Hebraising kind of text, was copied.[3]

Appendix I

Biblical Quotations in Inscriptions from the Aksumite Period

The earliest clear evidence for the existence of a translation into Geez of at least some parts of the Bible is provided, as we have already noted, by the occurrence of brief quotations from the Psalms, and from one or two other books, in three royal inscriptions that date from the first half of the sixth century. The quotations from the Psalter predominate, almost certainly because the psalms were used so much in the liturgy. I examined the significance of the psalm quotations in my contribution to *Der Septuaginta-Psalter und seine Tochterüber-setzungen,*[4] and the following discussion draws extensively on my contribution to that volume.

---

[1] Löfgren, *Daniel*, XLVII.

[2] Cf. Guidi, *Storia della letteratura etiopica*, 49–70.

[3] See above, p. 37 and n.1.

[4] Knibb, 'The Ethiopic Translation of the Psalms' [forthcoming].

The first of the royal inscriptions that concern us (RIÉth 191)[1] was found in Aksum and was set up by Kaleb, who reigned in the first half of the sixth century. The inscription begins with a quotation of Ps. 23:8b,[2] but contains no other biblical quotations. The inscription is written in Geez in South Arabian script, but the text of the psalm passage does not otherwise differ from the text in manuscripts of the Ethiopic Psalter (or in da Bassano's edition),[3] apart from reading ው·ስጠ፡ instead of the compound preposition በው·ስጠ፡ ('in').

The second inscription (RIÉth 195) was found at Marib in the Yemen and is attributed to Kaleb;[4] the text is in vocalised Geez. It contains in fragment 1 a quotation of Ps. 67:2 (lines 5–6), and in fragments 2–3 quotations of Ps. 65:16–17 and Ps. 19:8–9 (lines 21–23, 26–28) as well as a quotation of Matt. 6:33 and the beginning of a quotation from Isaiah (lines 19–21, 29).[5] The last of these breaks off

---

[1] For the text, see Bernand, Drewes, Schneider, Anfray, *Recueil des inscriptions de l'Éthiopie*, tome I, 271–74; tome II, planches 129–32; R. Schneider, 'Trois nouvelles inscriptions royales d'Axoum', *IV Congresso Internazionale di Studi Etiopici* (Accademia Nazionale dei Lincei, Problemi attuali di scienza e di cultura, Quaderno N. 191), Rome, 1974, Tomo I, 770–77, plates IV–VI.

[2] All references to the Ethiopic Psalter are given here according to the numbering of the Septuagint.

[3] For purposes of comparison I used Vat. Aeth. 4 (14th cent.) and BL Add. 18,994 (15th cent.) as representative of the oldest text of the Ethiopic Psalter accessible to us; but the Ethiopic text of the Psalter, unlike that of other biblical books, is relatively stable in the manuscript tradition, no doubt because of the use of the psalms for liturgical purposes. Cf. Müller, 'Zwei weitere Bruchstücke der Äthiopischen Inschrift aus Mârib', 69–70.

[4] For the text, see *Recueil des inscriptions de l'Éthiopie*, tome I, 284–88; tome II, planches 143–44; Müller, 'Zwei weitere Bruchstücke der Äthiopischen Inschrift aus Mârib', 59–74, Plates VIII–IX.

[5] Müller (see previous note) considers it possible that the inscription included quotations from other biblical passages in addition (for example (pp. 64–65), a citation from Gen. 15:7 in fragments 2–3, line 4). However, because of the damaged state of the inscription,

too soon for it to be of significance, and all the quotations are incomplete because of the fragmentary state of the inscription. The quotation of Ps. 19:8–9 appears to raise no difficulties — the greater part of the text has survived, the reconstruction is unproblematic, and the restored text corresponds to that of the manuscripts — but in the other cases there are omissions and/or other changes. Thus it is clear that the quotation of Ps. 65:16 did not include the equivalent of πάντες οἱ φοβούμενοι τὸν θεόν (Eth ኩልክሙ፡ እለ፡ ትፈርህዎ፡ ለእግዚአብሔር፡), and it is very likely that the quotation of Matt. 6:33 did not include any mention of 'the kingdom of the Lord' or 'his kingdom'. The quotation of Matt. 6:33 is also of interest because the text differs from that in the BFBS edition, but agrees with that in Abba Garima 3 (used here as a representative of the oldest accessible text);[1]

| 2–3, 20 | እንትሙስ፡ ቅድሙ፡ ኅሡ፡ ጽድ[ቀ፡ እግዚእ፡ ብሔር፡ ወዝንቱ፡ ኩሉ፡] |
| 2–3, 21 | ይትዌሰከክሙ፡ |

Literally, 'But you, do first (and) seek the righteous[ness of the Lord, and all this] will be added to you'.[2]

| AG 3 | ወአንትሙስ፡ ቅድሙ፡ ኅሡ፡ መንግሥቶ፡ ለእግዚእ፡ ብሔር፡ ወጽድቆ፡ ወዝሰ፡ ኩሉ፡ ይትዌሰከክሙ፡ |

---

not enough of the text of the suggested passages survives to be helpful in the present context.

[1] For the date of Abba Garima 3, see above, pp. 6–7 and n. 2 on p. 6. I have used this manuscript as a representative of the oldest text (and not Abba Garima 1) because a photocopy happened to be to hand.

[2] I follow the reconstruction of Müller ('Zwei weitere Bruchstücke', 62–63, 68–69; Müller transliterates the text, but I have used Geez characters as in the inscription). Müller notes as an alternative possibility for reconstruction '[his] righteous[ness and his kingdom, and all this]'; but however the text is reconstructed, it is clear that the word for 'kingdom' did not appear before the word for 'righteousness'.

Literally, 'But you, do first (and) seek the kingdom of the Lord and his righteousness, and all this will be added to you.

BFBS አንተሙሰ፡ ጎሡ፡ መቅድም፡ መንግሥተ፡ ዚአሁ፡ ወጽድቆ፡ ወዝንቱ፡ ኵሉ፡ ይትዌሰከከሙ፡

But you, seek first his kingdom and his righteousness, and all this will be added to you.

Both the inscription and Abba Garima 3, but not the BFBS edition, use the construction with the verb ቀደመ፡ to express the adverbial idea 'first'.[1] Finally, for Ps. 67:2 Müller has proposed, on the basis of his estimate of the number of letters and word-dividers in each line, a reconstruction in which the word for 'Lord' is omitted:

1, 6   ይ[ትነሣእ፡ ወይዘረዉ፡
                           ፀሩ፡]
1, 7   [ወይጕየዩ፡ ጸላእ]ቱ፡ እምቅድም፡ ገጹ፡ [
        May he arise, and may his enemies be scattered, and may his adversaries flee before his face.[2]

The omission of one word in the quotation of Ps. 67:2 does seem probable, but the possibility should also be considered that it was a word other than that for 'Lord'.[3]

The third, and by far the longest, of the three royal inscriptions (RIÉth 192) was found in Axum and was set up by Wa'zeb (W'ZB), the son of Kaleb.[4] It contains on the front side quotations of Ps. 17:48; 117:10; 34:1b–2; 34:4b–5; 17:38a + 40–41a; 117:15b–16a (lines 19–20, 25–26, 29–30, 30–31, 32–34, 34–35) as well as a quotation of Exod. 14:14 (lines 21–22) and a quotation of a passage I have been

[1] Cf. Dillmann, *Lexicon*, cols. 460–61.

[2] Müller, 'Zwei weitere Bruchstücke', 72–73.

[3] Müller himself notes that the distribution of his restorations on the two lines is purely hypothetical.

[4] For the text, see *Recueil des inscriptions de l'Éthiopie*, tome I, 274–78; tome II, planches 133–37; Schneider, 'Trois nouvelles inscriptions royales d'Axoum', *IV Congresso*, 777–86, plates VII–X.

unable to identify said to be from 'Ezekiel the prophet' (lines 18–19); the biblical quotations are all relatively well preserved, although the inscription is worn away in places and in general hard to translate. The inscription is in Geez in South Arabian script, and apart from orthographic and morphological differences as a result of this, there are some differences between the text of the psalm quotations and the text in the manuscripts:[1]

17:48a	በቀልየ ፡]	*lt bqly* (ሊተ ፡ በቀልየ ፡)
17:48b	በመትሕቴየ ፡]	*zmthty* (ዘመትሕቴየ ፡)
117:10a	ዐገተኒ ፡]	*'ktn* (ዐከተኒ ፡)
34:5b	ለይማቅዮሙ ፡]	*lysddm* (ለይስድዶሙ ፡)
17:40a	በፀብእ ፡]	*wst d[b]'* (ውስጠ ፡ ፀብእ ፡)
17:40b	ወአዕቀጽኮሙ ፡]	*w'wdqm* (ወአውደቆሙ ፡)

However, as will be apparent, the differences from what is found in the manuscripts are not very significant from a purely textual point of view: ሊተ ፡ በቀልየ ፡ for በቀልየ ፡ (17:48a), where ሊተ ፡ (= ἐμοί) is otiose;[2] difference of spelling (*k* instead of *g*, 117:10a); use of a different form (17:48b) and of a different preposition (17:40a), but with no change of meaning; and use of different verbs ('to drive away, to pursue' (ሰደደ ፡) for 'to afflict, torment' (ማቅየ ፡ , 34:5b); and 'to cause to fall' (አውደቀ ፡) for 'to entrap, to cause to stumble' (አዕቀጸ ፡ , 17:40b)). But apart from these differences, the text of the psalm passages in the inscription agrees with that of the text in the manuscripts.

[1] In the following list the text of Vat. Aeth 4 (corrected in one case against BL Add. 18,994) is given first.

[2] It is difficult to decide whether ሊተ ፡ was added in the inscription under the influence of the occurrence of the same word in the following line of the psalm or omitted from the text found in the manuscripts.

The text of Exod. 14:14 in the inscription corresponds to that in the edition of J. Oscar Boyd,[1] apart from the fact that twice it does not have the conjuntion **ወ**:

ወእግዚአብሔር ፡] *'gzbhr* (እግዚአብሔር ፡) OG κυριος

ወአንትሙስ ፡] *'tms* (አንትሙስ ፡) OG και υμεις

It is appropriate to refer here also to two other inscriptions. The first of these (RIÉth 250) was found at Saro in the region of Qohayto in Eritrea; it cannot be dated precisely, but belongs in the same general period as the three royal inscriptions we have just considered.[2] It consists of only three lines, which are almost entirely taken up by a quotation of what appears to be Ps. 139:2. The text is written in partially vocalised Geez, and the psalm passage reads (in vocalised form) as follows:

1   እብእሲ ፡ ዓማዒ ፡ አድኅነኒ ፡

2   ወባልሐኒ ፡ እብእሲ

3   ገፋዒ ፡

This may be compared with the text as given in Vat Aeth. 4 BL Add. 18, 994:

አድኅነኒ ፡ እግዚኦ ፡ እምብእሲ ፡ እኩይ ፡

ወእምሰብእ ፡ ዐማዒ ፡ ባልሐኒ ፡ ,

which, apart from the addition of the conjunction, is a literal rendering of the Greek:

Ἐξελοῦ με, κύριε, ἐξ ἀνθρώπου πονηροῦ,
ἀπὸ ἀνδρὸς ἀδίκου ῥῦσαί με.

Here, quite apart from orthographic differences, there are substantial differences between the text of the Saro inscription and the text of Ps.

---

[1] J. Oscar Boyd, *The Octateuch in Ethiopic.* Part II: *Exodus and Leviticus* (Bibliotheca Abessinica IV), Leiden and Princeton, 1911. Boyd's edition is based on Paris BN Éth. 102 (Zotenberg, no. 3), which, although attributed to the thirteenth century by Zotenberg, is to be dated to the end of the fourteenth or the beginning of the fifteenth century; see Uhlig, *Äthiopische Paläographie*, 41.

[2] For the text, see *Recueil des inscriptions de l'Éthiopie*, tome I, 336–37; tome II, planche 173. Cf. A.J. Drewes, *Inscriptions de l'Éthiopie antique*, Leiden, 1962, 29.

139:2 in the manuscripts: differences of word order; repetition of ብእሲ: instead of differentiation between ብእሲ: and ሰብእ: ; ዓማፂ: , not እኩይ: , for πονηρός, and ገፋኢ: , not ዐማፂ: , for ἄδικος. However, Drewes has pointed out that the first half of the inscription corresponds exactly to the Ethiopic text of Ps. 139:5b (ወእምብእሲ: ዐማፂ: አድኅነኒ:), and that the second half of the inscription is to be found in the Ethiopic version of Ps. 17:49c, but with a different word–order (እምብእሲ: ገፋኢ: ባልሐኒ:).[1] In view of this it may be suggested that the inscription contains not so much an 'archaic form' of Ps. 139:2, as Sergew Hable Sellassie suggested,[2] as a free quotation based on phrases from the psalms familiar from the liturgy.

The funerary inscription from Ham (RIÉth 232)[3] also deserves consideration here; it cannot be dated precisely, but has been attributed by Conti Rossini to the seventh-eighth century.[4] The inscription is in vocalised Geez and contains quotations of Job 14:1, John 6:54 and Isa. 26:19 (lines 6–8, 9–12, 13–15). The quotation from Isaiah is identical to the text found in Bachmann's edition[5] apart from the fact that it does not have the conjunction and particle attached to the first word:

---

[1] Drewes, *Inscriptions de l'Éthiopie antique*, 29. It is interesting to note that in Vat. Aeth. 4 ወእምሰብእ: has been altered to ወእምብእሲ: in 139:2b, but also that ወእምሰብእ: occurs for ወእምብእሲ: in 139:5b.

[2] Sergew Hable Sellassie, *Ancient and Medieval Ethiopian History*, 120.

[3] For the text, see *Recueil des inscriptions de l'Éthiopie*, tome I, 323–24; tome II, planche 165; Conti Rossini, 'L'iscrizione etiopica di Ham', *Atti della Reale Accademia d'Italia*, ser. vii, vol. 1, Rome 1939, 1–14.

[4] 'L'iscrizione etiopica di Ham', 13–14.

[5] J. Bachmann, *Der Prophet Jesaia nach der äthiopischen Bibelübersetzung*. I. Teil: *Der äthiopische Text*; II. Teil (not seen): *Der äthiopische Text in seinem Verhältnis zur Septuaginta*, Berlin, 1893. Bachmann's edition is based on Berlin Petermann II, Nachtr. 42 (15th cent.) and on Berlin Ms. orient. quart. 283 and Frankfurt Ms. orient. Rüppell II, 4.

ወምዉታነሰ ፦ (var. ሙታነሰ ፦) ይትነፐኍ ፦] ምዉታን ፦ ይትነፐኍ ፦
OG αναστησονται (+ γαρ A') οι νεκροι

However, the quotation of Job 14:1 differs from the text in the edition
of F.M. Esteves Pereira[1] (and of da Bassano) in two respects:

RIÉth 232 ብፁዕ ፦ ዘይትወለድ ፦ እምእንስት ፦ ዘሕጻጥ ፦ መዋዕሊሁ ፦

Blessed (is) the one born of a woman whose days (are)
few.

Pereira መዋቲ ፦ ዘይትወለድ ፦ እምእንስት ፦ ሕጻጥ ፦ መዋዕሊሁ ፦

The mortal born of a woman, his days (are) few.

The differences perhaps represent an adaptation of the passage to the
context of the funerary inscription.

A rather more significant alteration of the text occurred in the
case of John 6:54 in that the text in the inscription has been
harmonized with the text of John 8:52:[2]

RIÉth 232 ዘበሰዐ ፦ ሥጋየ ፦ ወሰቲየ ፦ ደምየ ፦ ኢይጥዕማ ፦ ለሞት ፦ ወአነ ፦
አነፐኍ ፦ አመ ፦ ደጋሪ ፦ ዕለት ፦

Whoever eats my flesh and drinks my blood shall not
taste death, but I will raise him on the last day.

This may be compared with the text of the relevant pieces of John
6:54 and 8:52 in Abba Garima 3:

John 6:54 ዘበሰዐ ፦ ሥጋየ ፦ ወሰትየ ፦ ደምየ ፦ ቦሕይወት ፦ ዘለዓለም ፦ ወአነ ፦
አነፐኍ ፦ በድጋሪት ፦ ዕለት ፦

Whoever eats my flesh and drinks my blood shall have
eternal life, and I will raise him on the last day.

John 8:52 ኢይጥዕሞ ፦ ለሞት ፦

Here it may be noted that, in contrast to Abba Garima 3 (and the
BFBS edition), the inscription treats ሞት ፦ as feminine and ዕለት ፦ as

---

[1] Esteves Pereira, *Le livre de Job: version éthiopienne*. Pereira's edition is based on Paris
BN Éth. 11 (Zotenberg, no. 7), which probably dates from about 1350 (see above, p. 18,
n. 3), and Paris BN Abb 55 (Conti Rossini, no. 12) from the fifteenth or sixteenth
century.

[2] As pointed out by Zuurmond (*Novum Testamentum aethiopice: The Synoptic Gospels*.
Part I, 37–38).

masculine and uses ኦም ፡ instead of በ for 'on'. But these differences are not significant, and the individual pieces of John 6:54 and 8:52 in the inscription correspond to the text of these passages in Abba Garima 3 (and the BFBS edition). Thus it appears that in the case of both Job 14:1 and John 6:54 + 8:52 we again have free quotation rather than evidence of an alternative (or earlier) form of the text.

In summary, the textual evidence provided by the quotations in the inscriptions is quite limited in extent, and it is important to keep this in mind in atempting to assess its significance. There are orthographic and morphological differences of various kinds between the text of the quotations and the text of the corrresponding passages in the manuscripts. But quite apart from differences of this kind, there are a number of, mostly minor, textual differences: non-occurrence of the conjunction ወ and the particle በ (RIÉth 192, 232), the occurrence of ለት ፡ in Ps. 17:48a (RIÉth 192), variations in the prepositions used, but with no change of meaning (RIÉth 191, 192, 232), and variations involving use of a different form or a different verb (RIÉth 192). More significantly the text has once or twice been quoted freely (the psalm passage in RIÉth 250, John 6:54 in RIÉth 232), and the omission(s) in RIÉth 195 should probably also be understood as (an) instance(s) of free quotation. It also seems likely that in one case (Job 14:1 in RIÉth 232) the biblical text was adapted to its context. But it is significant that the inscriptions do not provide evidence for the existence of an earlier form of the Ethiopic version quite different from that in the oldest Ethiopic manuscripts available to us. Rather they suggest that in the case of the Psalms the Ethiopic version essentially in the form known to us from the oldest manusripts was already in existence by the first half of the sixth century.[1] However, because of the very limited evidence at our disposal, it is not clear how far such a judgement would apply in the case of other books.

---

[1] Cf. Müller, 'Zwei weitere Bruchstücke', 69–70.

Translation Techniques

I

In an article published over a hundred years ago, August Dillmann, who among his many major achievements in the Ethiopic field edited a significant number of the books of the Ethiopic Old Testament, summed up the character of the Ethiopic version of the Bible as follows:

> Was nun den Charakter dieser Übersetzung betrifft, so ist sie sehr treu, gibt meist den griechischen Text wörtlich, oft bis auf die Stellung der Worte hinaus wider, kürzt nur hie und da scheinbar überflüssiges ab und ist im ganzen als eine sehr wohl gelungene und glückliche zu bezeichnen. Trotz aller Treue gegen den griechischen Text ist sie recht lesbar und, namentlich in den geschichtlichen Büchern, fliessend und trifft mit dem Sinn und den Worten des hebräischen Urtextes im A. T. oft auf überraschende Weise zusammen. Freilich finden in dem allem Gradunterschiede zwischen den einzelnen Büchern statt. Sehr gelehrte Leute waren allerdings die äthiopischen Übersetzer nicht und, wie es scheint, auch der griechischen Sprache nicht durchaus mächtig; namentlich wo es galt, seltenere Wörter und Sachnamen, sowie Kunstausdrücke zu übertragen, wird dies deutlich, und so haben sich, abgesehen von den vielen Fehlern, die aus der Mangelhaftigkeit ihrer griechischen Handschriften, und von den Unvollkommenheiten, die aus der verhaltnismäss-ig geringeren Reichhaftigkeit der äthiopischen Sprache ent-

sprangen, auch durch die Schuld der Übersetzer manche Miss-
verständnisse und Fehler eingeschlichen.[1]

There is no doubt about the essential validity of Dillmann's
comments, and since his time this judgement, or at least the second
part of it, has often been repeated. However, in order to form a
considered view of the character and accuracy of the Ethiopic
translation of the Old Testament, it seemed to me desirable to try to
look in a little detail at the way in which the Greek text was handled
by the translators. In recent years a number of scholars have attempted
studies of this nature, but with results of varying utility. In his edition
of the Ethiopic text of Hosea, Fuhs devoted a section of his
commentary to a description of the 'mode of working' of the
translator,[2] but his remarks, although sensible, are too brief to be of
real value. In the New Testament sphere, the late Josef Hofmann
attempted to analyse systematically the limitations of Ethiopic in
representing Greek and made a number of helpful observations, but
his comments at times need to be treated with caution.[3] Perhaps of
greatest utility is the description by Zuurmond of the character of the
oldest accessible Ethiopic text of the gospel of Mark, and many of his
remarks are also of relevance in an Old Testament context.[4] My own
intention is to consider, as a means of examining the translation
process, the question of how far the Ethiopic text provides a literal
translation of the Greek.

---

[1] Dillmann, 'Äthiopische Bibelübersetzung', *RE*[2] I (1877), 204.

[2] Fuhs, *Hosea*, 117–19.

[3] J. Hofmann, 'Limitations of Ethiopic in Representing Greek', in Metzger, *The Early Versions of the New Testament*, 240–56. Hofmann presents a useful overview, but makes some statements that are over-simplified and tends at times to treat the translation process too much as if it involved a system.

[4] Zuurmond, *Novum Testamentum aethiopice: The Synoptic Gospels*. Part I, 49–53. See also the comments of Hackspill ('Die äthiopische Evangelienübersetzung', 142–50) on the character of the Geez translation of Matthew in BN Éth. 22 (Zotenberg, No. 32).

Within the field of Septuagint studies there has over the last three decades been a considerable interest in translation technique, and this has generated a number of studies which, inasmuch as they are concerned with methodological issues, are also relevant to the Ethiopic Bible. These issues have been discussed by a number of scholars, but here particular reference should be made to the important paper by James Barr, *The Typology of Literalism in ancient biblical translations*, and to the essays by Anneli Aejmelaeus concerned with methodology that have been reprinted in her volume, *On the Trail of the Septuagint Translators.*[1] *Mutatis mutandis*, many

---

[1] J. Barr, *The Typology of Literalism in ancient biblical translations* (MSU XV = Nachrichten der Akademie der Wissenschaften in Göttingen, Phil.-Hist. Klasse, 1979, Nr. 11), Göttingen, 1979; A. Aejmelaeus, *On the Trail of the Septuagint Translators: Collected Essays*, Kampen, 1993 (see particularly the introduction (pp. 1–6), and the articles 'The Significance of Clause Connectors in the Syntactical and Translation-Technical Study of the Septuagint' (pp. 49–64), 'Translation Technique and the Intention of the Translator' (pp. 65–76), and 'What Can We Know about the Hebrew *Vorlage* of the Septuagint?' (pp. 77–115). Other recent studies of translation technique, in some cases reflecting significant differences of approach, include: S. P. Brock, 'Aspects of Translation Technique in Antiquity', *Greek, Roman and Byzantine Studies* 20 (1979), 69–87 (reprinted in *Syriac Perspectives on Late Antiquity*, London, 1984, chapter III); id., 'Translating the Old Testament', in D. A. Carson and H. G. M. Williamson (eds), *It is Written: Scripture Citing Scripture. Essays in Honour of Barnabas Lindars, SSF*, Cambridge, 1988, 87–98; E. Tov, 'The Nature and Study of the Translation Technique of the LXX in the Past and Present', in C. E. Cox (ed.), *VI Congress of the International Organization for Septuagint and Cognate Studies, Jerusalem 1986* (SCS 23), Atlanta, 1987, 337–59; id., *The Text-Critical Use of the Septuagint in Biblical Research* (Jerusalem Biblical Studies 8), Second edition, revised and enlarged, Jerusalem, 1997, 17–29; E. Tov and B. G. Wright, 'Computer-Assisted Study of the Criteria for Assessing the Literalness of Translation Units in the LXX', *Textus* 12 (1985), 149–87; B. G. Wright, *No Small Difference: Sirach's Relationship to its Hebrew Parent Text* (SCS 26), Atlanta, 1989, 19–118; G. Marquis, 'Word-Order as a Criterion for the Evaluation of Translation Technique in the LXX and the Evaluation of Word-Order Variants as

of the comments that they make also apply to the Ethiopic Bible, and equally much of what applies in the Ethiopic field is also of relevance to other ancient biblical translations. Two issues that affect the assessment of the Ethiopic Old Testament, but have a wider application, deserve to be mentioned here. On the one hand if we are to form a judgement about the character and accuracy of the Ethiopic translation, we need to know what Greek text lay before the translators,[1] but in any individual case we cannot be certain that we do know this. In practice, however, we ought to be able to form a fairly clear view overall of the type of text that was used for each book, and this should make it possible to form a reasonable judgement in individual cases. On the other hand for purposes of comparison we obviously must use the oldest Ethiopic text that we can recover, but we have to recognise that in any individual case this text may not represent the original translation, but may already have been subject to revision. The element of uncertainty seems to me to be much greater here. We can still form a judgement about the character and accuracy of the Ethiopic translation, but we have to recognise the uncertainties that affect that judgement.

Exemplified in LXX-Ezekiel', *Textus* 13 (1986), 59–84; I. Soisalon-Soininen, 'Beobachtungen zur Arbeitsweise der Septuaginta-Übersetzer', in *Studien zur Septuaginta-Syntax*. Zu seinem 70. Geburtstag am 4. Juni 1987 herausgegeben von A. Aejmelaeus and R. Sollamo (AASF B 237), Helsinki, 1987, 28–39; id., 'Methodologische Fragen der Erforschung der Septuaginta-Syntax', *Studien zur Septuaginta-Syntax*, 40–52; S. Olofsson, *The LXX Version: A Guide to the Translation Technique of the Septuagint* (Coniectanea Biblica, Old Testament Series 30), Stockholm, 1990. For other recent works on translation technique in the Septuagint, see C. Dogniez, *Bibliography of the Septuagint — Bibliographie de la Septante (1970–1993)* (Supplements to Vetus Testamentum 60), Leiden, New York, Köln, 1995, 47–52.

[1] Cf. Barr, *The Typology of Literalism*, 10: 'Most obviously, any decision about the literal or non-literal quality of a translated phrase depends upon the question of the *Vorlage*, the character of the original text that lay before the translator.' See further his discussion on pp. 10–14.

The Ethiopic Old Testament is fairly obviously characterized by a certain degree of consistency of rendering in both syntax and vocabulary, a consistency which, as in other cases, was no doubt adopted as a matter of convenience. But there is also apparent in some places a surprising lack of consistency, particularly in vocabulary, which is often hard to explain. It is clear that the translators were not rigidly following a system of translation, and the title 'Translation Techniques' given to this lecture is not meant to suggest that it is possible to identify any such system. It should be made clear that this is not a statistical study and does not for the most part draw on statistical surveys, although it is certainly concerned with very obvious features and trends in the Ethiopic text. Many of the topics discussed in this and the following lecture, for example the treatment of the Greek infinitive, deserve detailed examination, and in such studies statistics relating to the individual books of the Old Testament would have an important role to play. Such statistically-based studies are not, however, practical until there are reliable editions available for all the books of the Ethiopic Old Testament.[1] The evidence discussed in these lectures is derived from a detailed study of the Ethiopic text of Ezekiel and from extensive soundings made in other books of the Ethiopic Bible, particularly the prophetic literature, and what is intended is to see how the Greek was treated and what is the character of the resultant translation.

I wish in the present lecture to consider general aspects of the translation and questions of syntax, and in the final lecture to take up issues relating to vocabulary.

[1] For a list of the existing editions of the books of the Ethiopic Old Testament, see the bibliography.

II

The overwhelming impression created by the Ethiopic version of the Old Testament is one of literality. The translation is to a very great extent word for word, based on narrow segmentation of the text, and this is underlined by the way in which the Ethiopic very frequently follows the Greek and its word order almost slavishly, even at times to the point of unintelligibility.[1] The Ethiopic Old Testament is not of course the only literal ancient Bible translation, and significant parts of the Septuagint itself are also literal in character. Dillmann's remark that the Ethiopic translation often agrees in a surprising way with the sense and the wording of the Hebrew original is no doubt true, but the phenomenon to which he pointed is perhaps merely a reflection of the fact that the Ethiopic is a literal translation of what is itself quite a literal translation, and that for obvious reasons there are not infrequently similarities in vocabulary between the Ethiopic and the Hebrew.

One aspect of the Septuagint that has carried over into the Ethiopic translation and is a mark of its literal character is the widespread use of parataxis — with καί in the Septuagint, with the connecting particle ው in the Ethiopic. Parataxis with ው is, of course, a very common feature of the Ethiopic language, and in this case the Greek construction passed naturally into Ethiopic. In fact it is noticeable that the connecting particle ው is frequently inserted in the Ethiopic in places where the Greek does not have a conjunction, although in many cases the insertion may well be part of the inner-

---

[1] For examples of literal translation and of slavish following of the Greek word order, see Ezek. 7:13 ([all MSS except B 233] καὶ ἔτι ἐν ζωῇ τό ζῆν αὐτῶν· ὅτι ὅρασις εἰς πᾶν τὸ πλῆθος αὐτῆς [καὶ] οὐκ ἀνακάμψει, ወዓዲ፡ ውስት፡ ሕይወት፡ የሐይዎ፡ አስም፡ ርአይ፡ ውስት፡ ኵለንታሃ፡ ወኢተውዕጠ፡ አንከ፡) and 13:5 (οὐκ ἀνέστησαν οἱ λέγοντες Ἐν ἡμέρᾳ κυρίου, ወኢተንሥኡ፡ እለ፡ ይብሉ፡ በዕለት፡ አግዚአብሔር፡). Neither passage offers much sense in the Greek, at least in its context, but in both cases the Ethiopic follows the Greek fairly closely.

Ethiopic development of the text, and that the connecting particle ዐ is also occasionally used in places where the Greek has a causal conjunction (e.g. διότι, Ezek. 7:8(4)) or some other construction (e.g. τοῦ plus the infinitive, Jer. 1:8; ὡς plus the participle, Ezek. 8:17). In contrast it may be observed that sometimes the Ethiopic uses a subordinate construction where the Greek has parataxis with καί. The gerund is particularly used as a means of subordination, but other constructions are used as well. For example, in Ezek. 2:1 'and I saw (it), and I fell on my face (καὶ εἶδον καὶ πίπτω ἐπὶ πρόσωπόν μου)' becomes 'and seeing (it), I fell on my face (ወርእዮ ፡ ወደቁ ፡ በገጽየ ፡)'; and in Ezek. 4:8 'And behold, I put bonds on you, and you shall not turn (καὶ μὴ στραφῇς) from one side to the other' becomes 'And behold I will bind you that you may not turn (ከመ ፡ ኢትትመየጥ ፡) from one side to the other.'

The examples just discussed already illustrate at a simple level the kind of changes that have been made in the process of translation, sometimes apparently deliberately in order to accommodate the langauage of the Septuagint to the demands imposed by the Ethiopic language or simply to produce a smoother version, but sometimes for no obvious reason. Changes such as these mean that the translation, despite the overwhelming impression of literality, frequently differs in form from the underlying Greek and in this respect is not entirely literal. However — and this is the main point that I wish to make — it may be argued that where such changes were made primarily in response to the demands of the Ethiopic language, they did not normally affect the meaning of the text. Thus — to adopt a distinction drawn by Anneli Aejmelaeus — although the Ethiopic version in such cases does not provide a literal translation, it may nonetheless be thought to provide a faithful translation.[1] But changes that were grammatically conditioned could sometimes afffect the meaning; and

---

[1] Aejmelaeus, 'The Significance of Clause Connectors in the Syntactical and Translation-Technical Study of the Septuagint', *On the Trail*, 63: 'A distinction should be made between literalness and faithfulness. A good free rendering is a faithful rendering.'

the process of inner-Ethiopic development could then further lead to significant differences betwen the Greek and the Ethiopic, even in the oldest manuscripts that we possess.

This general point can be illustrated in relation to word order. The Ethiopic, as we have already observed, usually follows the word order of the Greek almost slavishly, but there is noticeable a tendency for the verb to be moved to the beginning of the sentence, where it would more naturally stand in Ethiopic (e.g. Ezek. 7:27; 8:12; 9:3). Normally changes in word order were neutral in effect, but the meaning could occasionally be affected, as has happened, for example, in Ezek. 11:21:

> καὶ εἰς τὴν καρδίαν τῶν βδελυγμάτων αὐτῶν καὶ τῶν ἀνομιῶν αὐτῶν, ὡς ἡ καρδία αὐτῶν ἐπορεύετο ('And to the heart of their abominations and of their transgressions, as their heart went');
>
> ወሐሩ፡ በልበ፡ ግየታቶሙ፡ ወኀጢአቶሙ፡ በከመ፡ ልቦሙ፡ ('And they walked according to the heart of their abominations and of their sins, in accordance with their heart').

The Greek text, which is closely modelled on the corrupt Hebrew, conveys little sense, and no doubt part of the reason for the movement of the verb in the Ethiopic to what must have seemed a more natural position was to make sense of the text. The change may have been made at a secondary stage, but in any case this is an instance where the change in the word order has led to a difference of meaning.[1]

---

[1] Cf. Ezek. 13:15: καὶ συντελέσω τὸν θυμόν μου ἐπὶ τὸν τοῖχον καὶ ἐπὶ τοὺς ἀλείφοντας αὐτῶν, πεσεῖται, ወእስልጥ፡ መዓትየ፡ ላዕለ፡ ይእቲ፡ አረፍት፡ ወትወድቅ፡ ላዕለ፡ እለ፡ ገርcዋ፡ . The movement of ትወድቅ፡ = πεσεῖται to before the euqivalent of ἐπὶ τοὺς ἀλείφοντας αὐτῶν has the effect that in the Ethiopic the wall, not God's wrath, falls on those who plaster it.

III

The general point that was made above may further be illustrated in relation to the treatment of nouns, where there are significant formal differences between the Greek and the Ethiopic. Thus there is noticeable within the Ethiopic version a tendency to use verbal in preference to nominal constructions, even in cases where Ethiopic had suitable nouns readily available. In Daniel 2, where the theme of the interpretation of Nebuchadnezzar's dream is central to the narrative, the word for 'interpretation' (σύγκρισις) occurs twelve times. In eight of the twelve cases the Ethiopic uses the noun ፍካሬ ፡ ,[1] which corresponds exactly in meaning to the Greek σύγκρισις; but in the remaining four cases, where there was no reason for change, it uses verbal constructions.[2] Again, it is well known that relative clauses are frequently used in Ethiopic as a periphrastic substitute for participles and adjectives, but they are also sometimes used in place of nouns. For example, ἐξιλασμός ('propitiation, atonement') appears in Ezek. 7:25 as ዘያሦ ር ቅ ፡ ('that which makes reconciliation'), Τίς ὑμῖν ἡ παραβολὴ αὕτη ('What (is) this proverb to you', Ezek. 12:22) becomes ምንት ኑ ፡ ዘይሜስሉ ፡ (literally 'What (is it) that they speak in a proverb?'), and τὴν βρῶσιν ὑμῶν καὶ τὴν πόσιν ὑμῶν ('your food and your drink', Dan. 1:10) becomes 'your food and what you drink' (ሲሳየክሙ ፡ ወዘተሰትዩ ፡). It is not obvious why a relative clause was used in any of these cases, but the meaning was not significantly affected.

The preference for verbal over nominal constructions is also exemplified by the way in which the Ethiopic version frequently uses

---

[1] Dan. 2:4, 7, 9, 24, 26, 30, 36, 45. The Ethiopic version of Daniel is based on the Theodotionic text (cf. Löfgren, *Daniel*, XLVII), and all quotations from, and references to, the Greek version of Daniel in these lectures are to this text.

[2] Dan. 2:5 (ወኢተፈክፉ ፡ ሊት ፡ , 'and (if) you do not interpret (it) to me'), 6a (ወፈከርክሙኒ ፡ ሊት ፡ , 'and (as soon as) you interpret (it) to me'), 6b (ወፈክፉ ፡ ሊት ፡ , 'and interpret (it) to me'), 16 (ወይፈክር ፡ ሎቱ ፡ , 'and would interpret (it) to him').

verbal forms where the Greek has the combination of preposition plus noun. Sometimes this occurs where the Greek has what may be regarded as an impersonal construction. For example, Ezek. 13:21 'and they will no longer be in your hands for perversion (εἰς διαστροφήν[1])' has been rendered in Ethiopic as 'and they will no longer fall into your hands that you may pervert them (ትገፍትእዎሙ፡)'. Similarly, in Ezek. 13:13 εἰς συντέλειαν ('for destruction') has been translated as ከመ፡ አጥፍቆሙ፡ ('that I may destroy them'). In cases such as these part of the reason for the change seems to have been the wish to make explicit the implied subject and object of the action described in the noun, that is, to clarify the meaning, and from this point of view the use of verbal forms may be said to represent the original faithfully. However, the same motive of clarification hardly applies in cases where the Greek uses the combination of preposition plus noun and the subject of the action is expressed. For example, in Dan. 11:3 'according to his will' (κατὰ τὸ θέλημα αὐτοῦ) has been translated as ዘፈቀደ፡ ('what he wished'), and in Jer. 1:3 'until the end (ἕως συντελείας) of the eleventh year of Zedekiah' has become 'until the eleventh year of the reign of Zedekiah was complete (እስከ፡ ተፈጸመ፡)'. In these kind of cases the meaning is unchanged, and there seems no obvious reason for the use of a different construction other than that the verbal construction was what instinctively seemed right to the translators.[2]

---

[1] So 534, whose reading the Ethiopic appears to presuppose here. But εἰς συστροφήν, the reading of all the other manuscripts, could well have been understood in the same way by the translator. Cf. 13:18bis (διαστρέφειν, ገፍትአ፡); 13:20a (συστρέφειν, ገፍትአ፡); 13:20b (ἐκστρέφειν, ገፍትአ፡).

[2] Cf. the remarks of Anneli Aejmelaeus ('Translation Technique and the Intention of the Translator', *On the Trail*, 65–76) on the role of intuition in the translation of the Septuagint, e.g. p. 66: 'But in fact, these translators never paused to consider their aims any more than the methods by which best to attain them. Their work is characterized by intuition and spontaneity more than conscious deliberation and technique.'

The instinctive adoption of what seemed normal was no doubt the reason for other similar changes that were made in the Ethiopic Old Testament in comparison with the Septuagint, such as the use of a verb on its own to render the combination of verb plus noun, or the expression of adverbial concepts by verbs. The former occurs very frequently in the Ethiopic Old Testament as, for example, in the case of phrases such as συνάπτειν πόλεμον ('to join battle', Dan. 11:25), for which the Ethiopic has simply ተቃተለ፡ ('to fight'), or διδόναι εἰς ἀφανισμόν ('to hand over to destruction' Ezek. 15:8), for which the Ethiopic has አጥፍአ፡ ('to destroy'[1]), or εἶναι ταπεινός ('to be lowly', Ezek. 29:14), for which the Ethiopic has ነሰረ፡ . The use of verbs to express adverbial concepts is a common feature of Ethiopic,[2] as it is of other Semitic languages, and so it is not unexpected that this phenomenon should occur in the Ethiopic Old Testament. For example, ἤδη ('already') is frequently rendered by by the verb ወድአ፡ ('to finish');[3] and the words κύκλῳ and κυκλόθεν ('around, all around'), although often rendered quite properly by forms of ዐውድ፡ used as an adverb, are sometimes rendered by the verbs ዐገተ፡ and ዖደ፡ (both meaning 'to surround').[4] In all these types of cases the

---

[1] Similarly τιθέναι εἰς ἔρημον (Ezek. 5:14), τιθέναι εἰς ἀφανισμόν (Ezek. 6:14), and εἶναι εἰς ἀφανισμόν (Ezek. 14:15) are rendered by አጥፍአ፡ .

[2] Cf. Dillmann, *Ethiopic Grammar*, 2nd edition, London, 1907 (reprinted Amsterdam, 1974), § 180.

[3] Cf. e.g. Susanna 55: ἤδη γὰρ ἄγγελος τοῦ θεοῦ λαβὼν φάσιν παρὰ τοῦ θεοῦ, ናሁ፡ ወድአ፡ መልአከ፡ እግዚአ፡ ብሐረ፡ ተአዘዘ፡ በገቦ፡ እግዚአ፡ ብሐረ፡ ('Behold, the angel of the Lord has already been commanded by the Lord').

[4] Cf. e.g. Ezek. 2:6: καὶ ἐπισυστήσονται ἐπὶ σὲ κύκλῳ, ወይተዉሙ፡ ላዕሌከ፡ ወየዐግቱከ፡ ('and they will rise up against you and surround you'); 40:16: καὶ ὡσαύτως τοῖς αιλαμ θυρίδες κύκλῳ ἔσωθεν, ወከማሁ፡ ለኢላም፡ መሳኮው፡ የዐውዱ፡ እንተ፡ ውስጡ፡ ('and likewise windows surrounded the "vestibule" on the inside'). — See also such passages as Ezek. 21:10: ὅπως σφάξῃς σφάγια, ከመ፡ ትርግዚ፡ ወትቀትል፡ ('that you may slaughter and kill'); 26:8: καὶ τὰς λόγχας αὐτοῦ ἀπέναντί σου δώσει, ወያረርብኪ፡ በኩያንዩሙ፡ ('and they will atack you with their spears').

Ethiopic does not represent exactly the form of the Greek, but it may be argued that the Ethiopic has faithfully represented the meaning of the Greek — except in cases where other changes also occurred. One such case occurs in Ezek. 19:8, where the Greek has 'and they set nations against him from lands round about' (καὶ ἔδωκαν ἐπ' αὐτὸν ἔθνη ἐκ χωρῶν κυκλόθεν). The Ethiopic version has 'and they sent nations against him from their lands to surround him' (ወፈነዉ᎓ አሕዛበ᎓ ላዕሌሁ᎓ ይዕግቶ᎓ እምበሐዉርቲሆሙ᎓). Here, as elsewhere, the verb 'to surround' (ዐገተ᎓) has been used with a pronouninal suffix to render κυκλόθεν. But other changes have been made, perhaps in the course of the transmission of the text, and the Ethiopic does not represent the meaning of the Greek.[1]

IV

Ethiopic, in common with other Semitic languages, has a considerably restricted system of 'tenses' and moods[2] in comparison with Greek, and in consequence it cannot reproduce exactly all the complexities of the Greek verbal system. Thus Ethiopic has to make do with two 'tenses' (the suffix and the prefix conjugation, i.e. the 'perfect' and the 'imperfect') and with two moods in the prefix conjugation (the indicative and the subjunctive); it cannot reproduce distinctions of tense in the Greek subjunctive and infinitve; it has no optative mood and only limited means of reproducing the Greek particle ἄν; and it suffers from a shortage of participial forms. For all these reasons the Ethiopic is not an exact reflection of the Greek in terms of its verbal

[1] For a comparable case, see Ezek. 7:22 where the Ethiopic ወይበዉአ᎓ ላዕሊሆሙ᎓ ወየደበይዮሙ᎓ ('and they will come upon them and surprise them') is quite different in meaning from the Greek καὶ εἰσελεύσονται εἰς αὐτὰ (sc. τὴν ἐπισκοπήν μου) ἀφυλάκτως ('and they will come upon it unguardedly').

[2] For the 'tenses' and moods in Ethiopic, and for their use in different types of clauses, see Dillmann, *Ethiopic Grammar*, §§ 88–90, 203–205.

system. This is, however, to a significant extent a matter of external form rather than of substance. The suffix and the prefix conjugation in Ethiopic have a range of meanings and are of course used in a quite different way from the Greek tenses; but their use is not arbitrary and, within the limitations imposed by the language, the Ethiopic does represent the tense distinctions of the Greek. Equally, although there is a tendency throughout the Ethiopic version towards simplification, Ethiopic does have the means of expressing the distinctions of meaning for which the Greek moods are used, and in broad terms the Ethiopic version has reproduced these distinctions of meaning. But what it is true to say is that in many cases it would not be possible to predict from the Ethiopic exactly which tense was used in the Greek. Thus, for example, in the absence of the Greek one could not tell whether an Ethiopic perfect reflected a Greek aorist or perfect,[1] or whether Ethiopic ከመ ፡ ('that') plus the subjunctive reflected Greek ἵνα or ὅπως with the subjunctive or Greek τοῦ plus the infinitive.[2]

The treatment of participles and infinitives may serve to illustrate what has just been said about the verbal system in general in that the treatment of these forms often involves significant changes in construction and hence of correspondence to the form of Greek. Normally, however, the meaning of the Greek is still faithfully

---

[1] A good illustration of this occurs in Ezekiel 18, where the perfect ሖረ ፡ is used for πεπόρευται (v. 9) and ἐπορεύθη (v. 11), and the perfect ገብረ ፡ is used for πεποίηκε (v. 12) and ἐποίησε (v. 13). Similarly in vv. 7–9, where the Greek has an aorist subjunctive and a sequence of future and perfect tenses, the Ethiopic uses only the perfect. In v. 15 it would be impossible to say, in the absence of other evidence, whether the Ethiopic በልዐ ፡ reflects βέβρωκε (so most MSS) or ἔφαγε(ν) (A''-403'-410), although in fact the latter is the more likely.

[2] Cf. e.g. Ezek. 37:23: ἵνα μὴ μιαίνωνται ἔτι (om. 410) ἐν τοῖς εἰδώλοις αὐτῶν, ከመ ፡ ኢይርኩሱ ፡ በግብፆሙ ፡ ('that they may not be defiled by their idols'); 36:30: ὅπως μὴ λάβητε (ἔτι) ὀνειδισμὸν λιμοῦ, ከመ ፡ ኢይሀሥሥዎሙ ፡ እንከ ፡ በረኃብ ፡ (literally, 'that they may never again insult you on account of famine'); and 29:15: τοῦ μὴ εἶναι αὐτοὺς πλείονας, ከመ ፡ ኢይብዝኁ ፡ ('that they may not increase').

reproduced in the Ethiopic. Participial constructions are frequently used in the Septuagint, but there is a comparative dearth of participles in Ethiopic, and many of the participles that do exist have lost their verbal force. In consequence participial constructions in the Septuagint have almost always been replaced[1] — by finite verbal forms,[2] or by gerunds,[3] or by circumstantial clauses (frequently introduced by እንዘ ፡ ('while') or some other conjunction),[4] or — in the case of the participle with the article — by relative clauses.[5] Similarly, although infinitives are very frequently used in the Septuagint, both as a translation of the Hebrew infinitive construct, but also in cases where the Hebrew does not have an infinitive,[6]

---

[1] Cf. Dillmann, *Ethiopic Grammar*, §§ 123, 181.

[2] Cf. e.g. Ezek. 13:6: βλέποντες ψευδῆ, μαντευόμενοι μάταια οἱ λέγοντες Λέγει κύριος, ሐሰተ ፡ ይሬእዩ ፡ ወያስገሉ ፡ ከንት ፡ ወይብሉ ፡ ይቤ ፡ እግዚአብሔር ፡ ('They see a lie and divine vanity and say, "Says the Lord"'); Susanna 13 καὶ ἐξελθόντες διεχωρίσθησαν ἀπ' ἀλλήλων, ወነ ፦ ወተፋለጡ ፡ በበይናቲሆሙ ፡ ('and they went away and separated from one another'). Cf. also the stereotyped use in Ezekiel of ወይቤለኒ ፡ ('and he said to me') to render (πρός με) λέγων (e.g. 15:1; 16:1; 17:1).

[3] Cf. e.g Ezek. 12:12: καὶ ὁ ἄρχων ... κεκρυμμένος ἐξελεύσεται, ወይወፅእ ፡ መልአክ ፡ ተኀቢኦ ፡ (literally, 'And the prince will go out, hiding himself').

[4] Cf. e.g. Ezek. 8:14: καὶ ἰδοὺ ἐκεῖ γυναῖκες καθήμεναι θρηνοῦσαι τὸν Θαμμουζ, ወረከብኩ ፡ እንስተ ፡ ይነብራ ፡ ወያስቀቅዋ ፡ ለተሙዝ ፡ (literally, 'And I found the women (as) they were sitting and weeping for Tammuz'); Susanna 39: καὶ ἰδόντες συγγινομένους αὐτούς, ወረከብናሆሙ ፡ ይሰክቡ ፡ ኅቡረ ፡ (literally, 'And we found them (as) they were lying together'); Ezek. 12:6: καὶ κεκρυμμένος ἐξελεύσῃ, ወትወፅእ ፡ እንዘ ፡ ትትኀባእ ፡ (literally, 'And you will go out while you hide yourself'); Susanna 45: καὶ ἀπαγομένης αὐτῆς ἀπολέσθαι, ወእንዘ ፡ ይወስዱ ፡ ይቅትልዋ ፡ (literally, 'And as they led (her) away to kill her').

[5] Cf. e.g. Ezek. 11:2: οὗτοι οἱ ἄνδρες οἱ λογιζόμενοι μάταια καὶ βουλευόμενοι βουλὴν πονηράν, እሉ ፡ ሰብእ ፡ እለ ፡ ከንት ፡ ይሔልዩ ፡ ወእኩየ ፡ ይመክሩ ፡ ('These (are) the men who devise vanity and plot evil'); 7:12: ὁ κτώμενος ... ὁ πωλῶν, ዘተማየጠ ፡ ... ዘሤጠ ፡ ('the one who buys ... the one who sells').

[6] For the infinitive in the Septuagint, see I. Soisalon-Soininen, *Die Infinitive in der Septuaginta* (AASF B 132,1), Helsinki, 1965.

infinitival forms are only occasionally used in the Ethiopic Old Testament.[1] Thus, for example, the Hebrew preposition ל plus the infinitive construct used in a final sense is most often rendered in Greek by the infinitive on its own or by τοῦ plus the infinitive.[2] The Ethiopic Old Testament does sometimes use the corresponding construction, namely the infinitive with or without the preposition ለ, as in Gen. 37:18: καὶ ἐπονηρεύοντο τοῦ ἀποκτεῖναι αὐτόν ('and they intended maliciously to kill him', or 'and they acted wickedly to kill him'), where the Ethiopic has as variant readings ወኣኅሰሙ፡ ለቀቲሎቱ፡ and ወኣኅሰሙ፡ ቀቲሎቱ፡ , which both reproduce the Greek construction. But far more frequently the Greek infinitive is translated by the subjunctive,[3] or by the the conjunction ከመ፡ ('that') plus the subjunctive,[4] or by some other means, including the conjunction ወ ('and') followed by the perfect, the imperfect or the subjunctive.[5] Again, the Hebrew preposition ב plus the infinitive construct, which is used primarily with a temporal meaning, is most often rendered in the Septuagint by ἐν τῷ plus the infinitive.[6] The Ethiopic Old Testament

---

[1] Cf. Dillmann, *Ethiopic Grammar*, §§ 182(b), 183, 203,2(a).

[2] Cf. Soisalon-Soininen, *Die Infinitive in der Septuaginta*, 49–54, 61, 75.

[3] Cf. e.g. Gen. 43:20: κατέβημεν τὴν ἀρχὴν πρίασθαι βρώματα, ወረድነ፡ ቀዲሙ፡ ንሢየተ፡ እክለ፡ .

[4] Cf. e.g. Gen. 43:18: ἡμεῖς εἰσαγόμεθα, τοῦ συκοφαντῆσαι ἡμᾶς καὶ ἐπιθέσθαι ἡμῖν, ያወስዱነ፡ ከመ፡ ይኩንዎን፡ (literally, 'they have brought us (in) that they might condemn us').

[5] Cf. e.g. Gen. 46:5: ἃς ἀπέστειλεν Ἰωσὴφ ἆραι αὐτόν, ዘፈነወ፡ ዮሴፍ፡ በዘያምጽእዎሙ፡ (literally, 'which Joseph had sent by which they might take them'); Ezek. 3:18: οὐδὲ ἐλάλησας τοῦ διαστείλασθαι τῷ ἀνόμῳ, ወኢነገርከ፡ ለኃጥእ፡ ወኢገሠጽከ፡ ('and you have not spoken to the sinner and have not warned him').

[6] For the renderings of ב plus the infinitive construct, see Soisalon-Soininen, *Die Infinitive in der Septuaginta*, 80–93, 188–90. Soisalon-Soinenen's analysis shows that overall in the Septuagint, but not in each individual book, ἐν τῷ plus the infinitive is used for ב plus the infinitve construct more frequently than all other renderings. It should

does occasionally use the corresponding construction, namely the preposition በ plus the infinitive. For example, in Gen. 19:33 and 35 (the story of Lot and his daughters — the wording is the same in both cases) the Greek has καὶ οὐκ ᾔδει ἐν τῷ κοιμηθῆναι αὐτὴν καὶ ἀναστῆναι ('and he did not know when she lay down or when she rose'), for which the Ethiopic reads ወኢያእመረ ፡ በሰኪቦታ ፡ ወበተንሥኦታ ፡ , exactly the same construction as in the Greek. But it is significant that of the twenty-two occurrences of ἐν τῷ plus the infinitive in Genesis — of which sixteen correspond to ב plus the infinitve construct, and six to other Hebrew constructions — it is only in 19:33 and 35 that the Ethiopic also uses infinitives. Rather in Genesis, as in the Ethiopic Old Testament as a whole, ἐν τῷ with the infinitive has almost everywhere been rendered either by a temporal clause, often introduced by ሶበ ፡ or አመ ፡ (both meaning 'when'), or — much less frequently — by a causal or a conditional clause or by some other kind of clause.[1]

One other aspect of the verbal system in the Ethiopic Old Testament should be mentioned, and that is the tendency to avoid the use of the passive.[2] Thus Greek passive forms have often been replaced by third person active forms used impersonally, and this type of construction is very familiar in Ethiopic and in other Semitic

---

be noted that ἐν τῷ plus the infinitive is also frequently used to render other constructions in Hebrew.

[1] Thus in Genesis — apart from 19:33, 35 — ἐν τῷ plus the infinitive has been renendered fifteen times by a temporal clause, twice by a causal clause, twice by a conditional clause, and once by a cohortative clause. The conjunctions used are as follows: ሶበ ፡ ('when': 9:14; 19:29bis; 24:52 (Hebrew כאשר + perfect); 38:28; 39:15 (Hebrew כ + inf. cstr.); 42:35 (Hebrew personal pronoun + participle)); አመ ፡ ('when': 35:1, 7); እንዘ ፡ ('while': 4:8; 32:25(26); 35:17, 18); እምድኅሬ ፡ ('after': 11:2); አምከመ ፡ ('as soon as': 44:31 (Hebrew כ + inf. cstr.)); እስመ ፡ ('because': 19:16 (Hebrew ב + noun)); ዘ ('because': 28:6); ለእመ ፡ ('if': 32:19(20); 34:15 (Hebrew ל + inf. cstr.)); ወ + subjunctive (34:22: ወንግዝር ፡ , 'Now let us circumcise').

[2] Cf. Dillmann, *Ethiopic Grammar*, § 192(c).

languages as a means of expressing the passive.[1] But sometimes Greek passive forms have been replaced by active forms, and the agent, or the implied agent, of the action in the Greek has been made the grammatical subject in the Ethiopic. Normally, such cases are straightforward, and the Ethiopic may be regarded as a faithful representation of the Greek, as in Ezek. 36:3, where the Greek Ἀντὶ τοῦ ἀτιμασθῆναι ὑμᾶς ... ὑπὸ τῶν κύκλῳ ὑμῶν τοῦ εἶναι ὑμᾶς εἰς κατάσχεσιν τοῖς καταλοίποις ἔθνεσι ('because you were shamefully treated by those around you so that you became the possession of the rest of the nations') has become እስመ፡ አገሱኩሙ፡ እለ፡ አውድክሙ፡ ከመ፡ ይኩንንክሙ፡ አሕዛብ፡ እለ፡ ተርፉ፡ ('because those around you treated you shamefully so that the rest of the nations took possession of you'). But, as we have seen elsewhere, other factors may in such cases lead to a change of meaning, as has happened, for example, in Ezek. 3:25:

ἰδοὺ δέδονται ἐπὶ σὲ δεσμοί, καὶ δήσουσί σε ἐν αὐτοῖς, καὶ οὐ μὴ ἐξέλθῃς ἐκ μέσου αὐτῶν ('Behold bonds have been put on you, and they will bind you in them, and you will not escape from them');

ናሁ፡ ሞቃሕኩከ፡ ወአሰርኩከ፡ ወኢትወፅእ፡ እማእከሎሙ፡ ('Behold I have fettered you, and I have bound you, and you will not escape from them').

The second clause in the Greek, which reflects the Hebrew וַאֲסָרוּךָ בָהֶם, itself uses an impersonal active construction, and the sense of the Greek is 'and you will be bound in them'. In the Ethiopic the first and second clauses have both been made active but also put into the first person to conform to the first person used in the following verse. This represents a definite shift in meaning, but the use of the first person

---

[1] Cf. e.g. Gen. 38:23: μήποτε καταγελασθῶμεν, ከመ፡ ኢይስሐቁ፡ ላዕሌነ፡ ('lest they laugh at us'); 38:24: ἀπηγγέλη τῷ Ἰούδᾳ, ዜነዉP፡ ለይሁዳ፡ ('they told Judah'); Ezek. 36:9: καὶ κατεργασθήσεσθε καὶ σπαρήσεσθε, ወገብሩክሙ፡ ወይዘርኡክሙ፡ ('and they will plough you and sow you'); 38:12: ἥ κατῳκίσθη, ገበ፡ ይነብሩ፡ አሕዛብ፡ ('where nations live').

may well belong to the inner-Ethiopic development of the text. Be that as it may, the consequence of these changes is that the third clause in the Ethiopic, the translation of which is quite literal, is unintelligible because there is no antecedent for the equivalent of ἐκ μέσου αὐτῶν.

V

The Ethiopic Old Testament differs considerably in extent from the Septuagint by way both of addition and omission, and this has an important bearing on the question of the literality of the text. The additions and omissions are present in the oldest form of the text accessible to us, but the possibility needs to be kept in mind that in many instances they represent a secondary development of the text and do not go back to the original translation. The additions are considerably fewer in number, and on the whole of much less significance, than the omissions. One major group of additions is represented by the cases in which a pronominal suffix has been attached to a noun or a verb as a means of making explicit the possessive pronoun or the direct object that is implied in the Septuagint.[1] The addition of the suffix in these cases is of neutral significance and certainly does not provide evidence that the translators had before them a Greek text which included the possessive pronoun or the direct object.

Another major group of additions is represented by those cases where a pronominal suffix has been attached to a noun, or a demonstrative pronoun has been inserted before a noun, or an

---

[1] Cf. e.g. Dan. 2:6: τὸ ἐνύπνιον ... τὸ ἐνύπνιον, ሕልምየ ፡ ... ሕልምየ ፡ ('my dream ... my dream'); 11:7: καὶ κατισχύσει, ወያጸንዖሙ ፡ ('and overpower them'). — For a recent study of additions of a comparable type in the Septuagint itself, see B. G. Wright, 'The Quantitative Representation of Elements: Evaluating "Literalism" in the LXX', in C. E. Cox (ed.), *VI Congress of the IOSCS*, 311–35.

anticipatory suffix has been attached to a word governing a noun and
ላ prefixed to the dependent noun, as a means of representing
explicitly the Greek definite article; this has happened because
Ethiopic does not possess an independent definite article or a special
form of the noun to indicate determination.[1] Again the addition of the
suffix or the insertion of the demonstrative in these cases if of neutral
significance from a textual point of view. An instructive example of
what is involved here is provided by Ezekiel's vision of the
destruction of Jerusalem (Ezek. 9–10) in which the angelic scribe seen
by the prophet is introduced in 9:2, according to the Greek and
Ethiopic versions, as 'a man clothed in linen with a girdle of sapphire
on his loins'. This figure is mentioned on six further occasions, on
four of which the Ethiopic has inserted a demonstrative meaning
'that' (ዝኩ፡ or ውእቱ፡) before the word for 'man'.[2] But in all six cases
the meaning is simply 'the man', and it seems to have been entirely an
arbitrary matter whether the demonstrative was inserted or not. In
none of these cases is a demonstrative used in the Greek. What
applies in the case of Ezekiel's 'man' provides a close parallel to a
rather more important case, that of the son of man figure in the
Parables of Enoch (1 Enoch 37–71), for which we only have available
an Ethiopic text. This figure is introduced in 1 Enoch 46:1, beside the
'one who had a head of days', as 'another, whose face had the
appearance of a man, and his face (was) full of grace, like (that) of
one of the holy angels'. Thereafter in the Parables the expression 'son
of man' is used to refer to this figure, and sometimes the
demonstrative has been placed before the expression 'son of man',[3]

---

[1] Cf. Dillmann, *Ethiopic Grammar*, § 172.

[2] Ezek. 9:11; 10:3, 6, 7; the passages without the demonstrative are 9:3; 10:2.

[3] The demonstratives used are as follows: ዝኩ፡ ('that'): 46:2; 48:2; 62:5, 9, 14; 63:11;
ውእቱ፡ ('that'): 69:26, 29bis (in the first case omitted by two of the manuscripts with the
older type of text); 70:1; ዝንቱ፡ ('this'): 46:4. In 69:27, although there is no
demonstrative, the phrase 'son of man' has been made definite by the use of an
anticipatory suffix.

and sometimes not.[1] However, in all cases it seems to me that the meaning is 'the son of man', and no great significance can be attached to the presence or the absence of the demonstrative — as has at times been suggested.[2]

The remaining additions, which perhaps rather more than the pronominal suffixes and demonstrative pronouns considered so far properly deserve to be called 'additions', consist for the most part of single words and form a somewhat miscellaneous collection. In some cases the additions have been made under the influence of the

---

[1] No demonstrative is used in 46:3; 62:7; 71:14. In 46:3 and 71:14 ወኣኅተ ፡ does occur, but in both cases as a means of expressing the verb 'to be'.

[2] Cf. e.g. M. D. Hooker, *The Son of Man in Mark*, London, 1967, 44: 'While it is possible that the demonstrative may merely represent the Greek definite article, it seems unlikely that this is a sufficient explanation here. Not only does the "this" refer back to the one "whose countenance had the appearance of a man", but its use is in striking contrast to the absence of any comparable demonstrative with "Elect One"'; M. Black, *The Book of Enoch or I Enoch* (Studia in Veteris Testamenti Pseudepigrapha 7), Leiden, 1985, 206: 'It has been frequently pointed out that the demonstrative adj. corresponds to the Greek definite article ... At the same time, the demonstratives are, for the most part, required in Eth. to indicate unequivocally that it is no ordinary "son of man" that is meant — they mean "ille homo".' — From a different perspective J. J. Collins ('The Son of Man in First-Century Judaism', *New Testament Studies* 38 (1992), 455–57) has suggested that the absence of the demonstrative in 1 Enoch 71:14, in which Enoch himself is aparently identified as the son of man, is significant for the interpretation of the passage; but cf. Knibb, 'Messianism in the Pseudepigrapha in the Light of the Scrolls', *Dead Sea Discoveries* 2 (1995), 179.

immediate context[1] or of similar formulations in parallel passages.[2] In some cases obvious details have been supplied[3] or explanatory glosses have been inserted.[4] In some cases words which have little significance in their context, such as 'all' (Ezek. 3:15) or 'behold' (Ezek. 2:3), have been added. And in some cases the additions are the result of attempts to 'improve' passages,[5] or are the result of error of various kinds.[6] It is likely that many, if not the majority, of these additions were made during the course of the transmission of the text and do not go back to the original translation; but, whatever their origin, they detract from the Ethiopic version in terms of it being a literal representation of the Greek text.

[1] Cf. e.g. Ezek. 1:4: καὶ πῦρ ἐξαστράπτον] + እምኔሁ፡ ('from it'); 7:5(8): πάντα τὰ βδελύγματά σου] ኵሎ፡ ፍኖትኪ፡ ወርኵስኪ፡ ('all your ways and your abominations'); 16:13: σεμίδαλιν καὶ ἔλαιον καὶ μέλι (καὶ μέλι καὶ ἔλαιον O' L" ... 106) ἔφαγες] ወሐረስኩኪ፡ በስንጻሊ፡ ወበመዓር፡ ወበቅብእ፡ ወተሴሰይኪ፡ ወበላዕኪ፡ ወሰባሕኪ፡ ('And I fed you with fine flour and honey and oil, and you fed and ate and grew fat').

[2] Cf. e.g. Ezek. 2:1, 3: Υἱὲ ἀνθρώπου] pr. አንተ፡ ('you'; cf. vv. 6, 8); 7:26: καὶ βουλὴ ἐκ πρεσβυτέρων] ወትረሳዕ፡ ምክር፡ እምሊቃውንት፡ ('and counsel vanishes from the elders'; cf. Jer. 18:18, and Knibb, JSS 33 (1988), 25).

[3] Cf. e.g. Ezek. 13:7: καὶ ἐγὼ οὐκ ἐλάλησα (all MSS except B)] ወአነ፡ አግዚአብሔር፡ ኢነበብኩ፡ ('and I, the Lord, have not spoken'); Dan. 1:17: καὶ ἐνυπνίοις] ወፍካሬ፡ ሕልም፡ ('and the interpretation of dreams'); 1:21: Κύρου τοῦ βασιλέως] pr. መንግሥቱ፡ ለ ('of the reign').

[4] Cf. e.g. Ezek. 13:19: ἕνεκεν δρακὸς κριθῶν] በአንተ፡ ሕፍሮሙ፡ ምልአ፡ ሕፍን፡ ሰገም፡ ('for the sake of their bribe, a handful of barley').

[5] Cf. e.g. Ezek. 7:23: διότι] + ከመ፡ ('as', 'for as the land is full of peoples, (so) the city is full of lawlessness'); 7:26: οὐαὶ ἐπὶ οὐαὶ ἔσται] pr. ዘእንበላ፡ ('But'); 11:15: ἡμῖν δέδοται ἡ γῆ] pr. አስመ፡ ('because').

[6] Cf. e.g. Ezek. 10:19: ἐπὶ τὰ πρόθυρα τῆς πύλης] + ጸዳ፡ ('outer'); 13:6: καὶ ἤρξαντο τοῦ ἀναστῆσαι λόγον] + ወይብሉ፡ ('and they say'); Dan. 1:3: καὶ ἀπὸ τοῦ σπέρματος τῆς βασιλείας] ያምጽአ፡ እምዘመደ፡ መንግሥት፡ ('(and) to bring some of the royal family').

VI

The same is true to a considerably greater extent of the numerous omissions.[1] Some of these are undoubtedly the result of carelessness, or of the deliberate abbreviation and adjustment of the text during the course of its transmission. There are many small omissions of this kind, and the major abbreviation of the text of 1 Enoch 83–108 that occurs in Abbadianus 55[2] is no doubt also to be explained in the same way.

However, in addition to omissions that were the result of carelessness in the transmission of the text or of deliberate abbreviation, there are many that may well go back to the original

[1] The following list of omissions from Ezekiel 1 is given as an illustration of the overall extent of the omissions in the Ethiopic Old Testament:

2	τὸ πέμπτον
4	καὶ ἰδού
	ἐξαῖρον
10	ὁμοίωσις τῶν προσώπων αὐτῶν
	τοῖς τέσσαρσι (2°)
12	πορευόμενον
17–18	αὐτὰ οὐδ'
	αὐτά, καί
19	τὰ ζῷα
22	ὁμοίωμα
24	ὡς φωνὴν ἱκανοῦ ἐν τῷ πορεύεσθαι αὐτά
26	τοῦ ὁμοιώματος
	ὁμοίωμα (2°)
27	ὁράσεως
	καὶ ἀπὸ ὁράσεως ὀσφύος καὶ ἕως κάτω εἶδον
28	ὅταν ᾖ

[2] Cf. R. H. Charles, *The Ethiopic Version of the Book of Enoch* (Anecdota Oxoniensia, Semitic Series XI), Oxford, 1906, xx, xxiv; Knibb, *The Ethiopic Book of Enoch*, vol. 1, xii.

translation. Some of these are individual words or short phrases which appear to have been deemed superfluous to the sense — as, for example, in the following cases:

Ezek. 3:11 εἰς τὴν αἰχμαλωσίαν πρὸς τοὺς υἱοὺς τοῦ λαοῦ σου] om. πρὸς τοὺς υἱούς Eth.

Ezek. 3:15 καὶ εἰσῆλθον εἰς τὴν αἰχμαλωσίαν μετέωρος καὶ περιῆλθον τοὺς κατοικοῦντας ἐπὶ τοῦ ποταμοῦ τοῦ Χοβαρ τοὺς ὄντας ἐκεῖ] om. μετέωρος and τοὺς ὄντας ἐκεῖ Eth.

Dan. 1:3 καὶ ἀπὸ τῶν φορθομμιν (‏וּמִן־הַפַּרְתְּמִים‎, 'and from the nobles')] om. Eth.

Dan. 2:14 τότε Δανιηλ ἀπεκρίθη βουλὴν καὶ γνώμην τῷ Αριωχ] om. βουλὴν καὶ γνώμην Eth.

In Dan. 1:3 the omission may have been partly because the phrase was not understood by the translators.

It is perhaps of interest to refer here to another instance of this kind in view of the fact that the Greek translation of the original Hebrew phrase was discussed by Barr in his *The Typology of Literalism in ancient biblical translations*.[1] The idiomatic expression 'to break the staff of bread' (‏שׁבר מטּה־לחם‎) occurs five times in the Hebrew Bible and once in Ben Sira. In four of these passages (Ps. 104:16; Ezek. 4:16; 5:16; 14:13) the expression was translated literally into Greek as συντρίβειν στήριγμα ἄρτου, and in two (Lev. 26:26; Sir. 48:2) a free translation was given. The Ethiopic follows the Greek in both the literal and the free[2] translations, but it is the treatment of στήριγμα ἄρτου in the literal translations that is of concern here. In two passages the word for 'staff' was omitted in the Ethiopic translation, and in the other two it is represented not by the word 'staff', but by a paraphrase, ኀይል ('strength'):

Ezek. 4:16: ἰδοὺ ἐγὼ συντρίβω στήριγμα ἄρτου

---

[1] Barr, *The Typology of Literalism*, 23–24.

[2] Lev. 26:26: ἐν τῷ θλῖψαι ὑμᾶς σιτοδείᾳ ἄρτων, ሶበ፡ ኣኅሥምክሙ፡ ኀይል፡ ኅብል፡ ; Sir. 48:2: ὃς ἐπήγαγεν ἐπ᾽ αὐτοὺς λιμόν, ወአምጽአ፡ ርኁበ፡ ላዕሌሆሙ፡ .

ናሁ፡ አነ፡ ኣጠፍእ፡ እክለ፡ [1]

Ezek. 5:16 καὶ συντρίψω στήριγμα ἄρτου σου

ወኣጠፍእ፡ እክለኪ፡

Ezek. 14:13 καὶ συντρίψω αὐτῆς στήριγμα ἄρτου

ወእቀጠቅጥ፡ ጎይለ፡ እክላ፡

Ps. 104:16 πᾶν στήριγμα ἄρτου συνέτριψεν

ወእጥፍእ፡ ኩሎ፡ ጎይለ፡ እክለ፡

In some instances the omission of individual words and phrases is linked with the simplification and smoothing out of the text, and here too it seems to me that there are, in some cases at least, reasonable grounds for thinking that the omissions go back to the original translation. A striking example of this occurs in Dan. 2:29 where the Greek, which mirrors the Aramaic exactly, reads βασιλεῦ, οἱ διαλογισμοί σου ἐπὶ τῆς κοίτης σου ἀνέβησαν ('O king, your thoughts on your bed went up'). This appears in the Old Ethiopic version as ንጉሥ፡ እስመ፡ ጎለይክ፡ ('O king, because you thought'), on which Löfgren appositely commented: 'frei und stark abkürzend gegenüber den übrigen Zeugen.'[2] The Ethiopic has in fact omitted ἐπὶ τῆς κοίτης σου as well as treating the awkward Greek phrase οἱ διαλοισμοί σου ἀνέβησαν very freely in an attempt to produce a smoother text.

Apart from the numerous omissions of individual words and short phrases, major omissions and substantial abbreviation of the text are to be found towards the end of a number of books. Thus major omissions occur in chapter 52 of the Old Ethiopic text of Jeremiah,[3] in chapter 11 of the Old Ethiopic text of Daniel,[4] and in chapters 42–48

[1] In this instance the word for 'staff' (በትር፡, hence በትረ፡ እክለ፡) was inserted as a correction in Abbadianus 35.

[2] Löfgren, *Daniel*, 105.

[3] Cf. Schäfers, *Die äthiopische Übersetzung des Propheten Jeremias*, 64–71; the omissions consist of a couple of words at the end of v. 18 and the whole of vv. 19–34.

[4] Cf. Löfgren, *Daniel*, XXXIX.

of the older text of Ezekiel.[1] Schäfers has plausibly argued from a comparison of the two later versions of the Ethiopic text of Jeremiah 52 that the omitted passage did not form part of the Old Ethiopic translation, and he suggests that the person who translated Jeremiah deliberately left out the passage because he did not properly understand it.[2] A similar argument could well be made in the case of the major omissions at the end of Ezekiel and Daniel, but in these cases it seems to me that the evidence is less certain.

VII

The case of Dan. 2:29, discussed above, brings us very clearly into the realm of free translation. Free translation properly so called presupposes that the translator, as in the example just discussed, did have a more or less correct understanding of the original text, but chose for whatever reason not to express it in literal terms. Translation of this kind is to be found frequently in the Ethiopic Old Testament. It is often associated with attempts to simplify the underlying text, and the occurrence of additions and omissions is itself of course one aspect of a free style of translation. Choice of vocabulary is also an important area where the distinction between free and literal translation can be observed, and this aspect will be considered further in the final lecture. But free translation may result from the fact that the translator did not have a proper understanding of the original text and in this case can become what is at best described as a guess.[3]

---

[1] Cf. Knibb, *JSS* 33 (1988), 23; id., *JSS* 34 (1989), 446. A systematic survey of older manuscripts of the entire Ethiopic Old Testament would probably reveal other examples of this kind.

[2] Schäfers, *Die äthiopische Übersetzung des Propheten Jeremias*, 66: 'Da er aus der LXX übersetzte, vermochte er, da er wohl nicht hebräisch verstand oder die zahlreichen transkribierten hebräischen Worte in der LXX, die nun folgen, nicht als solche erkannte, keine Übersetzung des folgenden zu bieten.'

[3] Cf. Barr, *The Typology of Literalism*, 13–16.

Free translation is, not surprisingly, often found in the Ethiopic Old Testament where the Greek, because of its dependence on, and frequent misunderstanding of, the Hebrew, is awkwardly or obscurely expressed, as, for example, in Ezek. 14:4 where the Ethiopc text is a paraphrase of the Greek:

> ἐγὼ κύριος ἀποκριθήσομαι αὐτῷ (+ ἐν αὐτοῖς all MSS except B A 534) ἐν οἷς ἐνέχεται ἡ διάνοια αὐτοῦ ('I, the Lord, will answer him for the things in which his mind has become entangled');
>
> ኣነ ፡ እግዚኣብሔር ፡ እወሥእኵ ፡ በላዕሊሆሙ ፡ ዘሐለየ ፡ በልቡ ፡ ('I, the Lord, will answer him for the things which he thought in his heart').

Usually, as in this case, it is not difficult to see why there might have been a temptation to paraphrase the text, but not always. In Dan. 2:6 Nebuchadnezzar promises the wise men that if they reveal to him his dream and its interpretation, they will receive great rewards, but the Ethiopic version of the promise differs somewhat surprisingly from the Greek:

> δόματα καὶ δωρεὰς καὶ τιμὴν πολλὴν λήμψεσθε παρ' ἐμοῦ ('gifts, and presents, and great honour, you will receive from me');
>
> ትነሥኡ ፡ ፍትሐክሙ ፡ ወዐስበክሙ ፡ ወብዙኅ ፡ ኣክብረክሙ ፡ (literally, 'you will receive your gifts and your presents, and I will honour you greatly').

The Greek is perfectly straightforward, and it might have been expected that it would have been translated quite literally, but instead the Old Ethiopic text reveals some significant changes. The movement of the verb to the beginning and the addition of the pronominal suffixes are not unusual, but there seems no reason whatsoever for the change of construction at the end, unless it is to be explained as inner-Ethiopic development.

VIII

There are also of course numerous instances of mistranslation within the Ethiopic Old Testament. Sometimes these mistakes are at least understandable, even if they do not reflect well on the ability of the translators, as for example in Ezek. 26:10–11 where the text was completely misunderstood because the relatively rare form ὁπλαῖς ('hooves') was misread as ὅπλοις ('weapons').[1] But the mistranslation that is found in Ezek. 40:10 as a result of the misreading of ἕν, the neuter form of the Greek numeral 'one', as ἐν, the preposition 'in', is much harder to justify.[2] It is of interest, however, that a comparable mistake occurs in Mark 4:8, where εἷς, the masculine form of the numeral 'one', was misread as εἰς, 'into'.[3]

The distinction between free translation and mistranslation is usually clear-cut, but there are inevitably cases where the distinction between the two is blurred. The complexities that can sometimes be involved are well illustrated by two closely related passages in Daniel 2.

The account of Nebuchadnezzar's dream and its interpretation (Dan. 2:1) begins, in the Greek and in the Ethiopic respectively, as follows:

---

[1] Ezek. 26:10bβ–11a: εἰσπορευομένου αὐτοῦ τὰς πύλας σου ὡς εἰσπορευόμενος εἰς πόλιν ἐκ πέδιου. ἐν ταῖς ὁπλαῖς τῶν ἵππων αὐτοῦ καταπατήσουσι πάσας τὰς πλατείας σου, ወይበውኡን፡ ለአናቅጽኪ፡ ከመ፡ ይበውእ፡ አዕጻተ፡ ሐቅል፡ በንዋየ፡ ሐቅል፡ ወይኬድ፱፡ አፍራሲሁ፡ መርሕበኪ፡ ('and he will enter your gates as one enters country villages with weapons. His horses will trample your broad places').

[2] Ezek. 40:10: καὶ μέτρον ἕν τοῖς τρισι καὶ μέτρον ἐν τοῖς αιλαμ ἔνθεν καὶ ἔνθεν, ወዐቅም፡ ውስት፡ wለስቲሆሙ፡ ወዐቅም፡ ውስት፡ ኤላም፡ አምነሌ፡ ወአምነሌ፡ ('and (there was) a measure in the three of them, and (there was) a measure in the "vestibules" on either side').

[3] Cf. Zuurmond, *Novum Testamentum aethiopice: The Synoptic Gospels*. Part I, 50, 125; Part II, 353. (Part I, p. 125 should read 'the translator misread εἷς as εἰς', not 'the translator misread εἷς for εἰς; there is a similar error in Part II, p. 353.)

Ἐν τῷ ἔτει τῷ δευτέρῳ τῆς βασιλείας ἠνυπνιάσθη
Ναβουχοδονοσορ ἐνύπνιον, καὶ ἐξέστη τὸ πνεῦμα αὐτοῦ,
καὶ ὁ ὕπνος αὐτοῦ ἐγένετο ἀπ' αὐτοῦ ('In the second year of
(his) reign, Nebuchadnezzar dreamed a dream, and his spirit
was disturbed, and his sleep left him');

በካልእ ፡ ዓመት ፡ ዘመንግሥቱ ፡ ሐለመ ፡ ናቡከደነጾር ፡ ሕልመ ፡
ወደንገፀት ፡ መንፈሱ ፡ ወረስዐ ፡ ሕልሞ ፡ ('In the second year of
his reign, Nebuchadnezzar dreamed a dream, and his spirit was
disturbed, and he forgot his dream').

The Ethiopic version of the first part of Dan. 2:1, apart from the
obvious addition of a pronominal suffix, is completely literal, but in
the final clause we appear to have a straight mistranslation. In fact, as
Löfgren noted, the translator took the word ὕπνος ('sleep') to be the
same as ἐνύπνιον ('a dream'),[1] and it can be argued that 'and he
forget his dream', although free, well conveys the sense of 'and his
dream left him'. The interpretation given to Dan. 2:1 has then carried
over into Dan. 2:3:

καὶ εἶπεν αὐτοῖς ὁ βασιλεύς Ἡνυπνιάσθην (+ ἐνύπνιον Q*-
233' L'-88), καὶ ἐξέστη τὸ πνεῦμά μου τοῦ γνῶναι τὸ
ἐνύπνιον ('And the king said to them, I dreamed (a dream), and
my spirit was disturbed to know the dream ');

ወይቤሎሙ ፡ ንጉሥ ፡ ሐለምኩ ፡ ሕልመ ፡ ወደንገፀት ፡ ነፍስየ ፡ ወረሳዕኩ ፡
ሕልምየ ፡ ('And the king said to them, I dreamed a dream, and
my spirit was disturbed, and I forgot my dream').

In the last clause the Ethiopic again appears at first sight to give a
straight mistranslation of the Greek. However, the origin of the
Ethiopic, as Löfgren observed, seems to lie in the fact that the
translator took τοῦ γνῶναι ('to know') not in a final sense, but as a
genitive of separation dependent on ἐξέστη ('from knowing').[2] It can
be argued that the Ethiopic 'and my spirit was disturbed, and I forgot
my dream' is a reasonable free translation of the Greek understood as

[1] Cf. Löfgren, *Daniel*, 102.

[2] Cf. Löfgren, *Daniel*, 103.

'and my spirit was disturbed from knowing the dream.' We thus appear to have here two instances of free translation dependent on a prior misunderstanding of the text, in effect a combination of free translation and mistranslation. But the question has to be asked whether the text really was misunderstood, and whether the Ethiopic translation does not rather represent a deliberate reinterpretation of the Greek. The interpretation given in the Ethiopic fits in well with the rest of the story, and a comparable understanding of the text of verses 1 and 3 can be found in the Vulgate.[1]

Normally within the Ethiopic Old Testament in cases of free translation and mistranslation it is possible, albeit sometimes with difficulty, to see how the translation has come about, and indeed, as Barr has reminded us,[2] the useful employment of terms such as 'free translation' is dependent on our being able to trace some kind of semantic path between the translation and the original. But there are cases within the Ethiopic Old Testament where it is very difficult to see any kind of connection with the Greek text. In Dan. 2:8 Nebuchadnezzar's complaint to the wise men: καιρὸν ὑμεῖς ἐξαγοράζετε ('you are seeking to gain time'), is not cast in obscure Greek, and the sentence was rendered perfectly adequately in one late Ethiopic manuscript as አንትሙ ፡ ተጋፖሙ ፡ ዕድሜ ፡ . But the Old Ethiopic text of Daniel has ታስተገፍሩኒ ፡ ('you are treating me with contempt'), and in a case such as this it is almost impossible to explain the origin of the text.

IX

To try to summarise what I have been saying, my concern in this lecture has been with the character of the Ethiopic translation, with broad trends in the way in which the Greek text was handled by the

---

[1] The parallels are noted by Löfgren.

[2] Barr, *The Typology of Literalism*, 13.

translators. Inevitably I have been concerned with differences, not similarities, and I have taken no account of the ways in which the Ethiopic frequently mirrors the Greek closely. The Ethiopic Old Testament is overwhelmingly a literal translation, but in its wording and construction it often differs from the Greek quite strikingly, sometimes because of the need to take account of the distinctive features of the Ethiopic language, but sometimes for no obvious reason. However, the changes that have been introduced, where they have been made primarily in response to the needs of the Ethiopic langauge, have not normally resulted in significant differences of meaning except where other factors also intervened, whether at the time of the original translation or by way of inner-Ethiopic development. The translation is also characterized by numerous additions and omissions, but these, insofar as they were not caused by grammatical considerations, largely belong to a secondary stage in the development of the text; but there are some omissions which may well go back to the original translation. There are in addition numerous instances of free translation and some of mistranslation.

A study of this nature raises the question of the extent to which it is possible to reconstruct the Greek version from the Ethiopic translation for text-critical purposes. This question was specifically addressed by J.R. Miles in his book *Retroversion and Text Criticism: The Predictability of Syntax in an Ancient Translation from Greek to Ethiopic*.[1] Miles compiled statistics of the ways in which the Greek constructions used in Esther 1–8 were rendered in Ethiopic, and on the basis of these statistics attempted to predict the Ethiopic syntax of Esther 9 from the Greek, and the Greek syntax of Esther 10 from the Ethiopic. He also tested his results on the Greek text of chapter 3 of Esdras b[2] and the Ethiopic version of 4 Baruch 1. Miles had the very

---

[1] J. R. Miles, *Retroversion and Text Criticism: The Predictability of Syntax in an Ancient Translation from Greek to Ethiopic* (SCS 17), Chico, 1985.

[2] Esdras b (Ezra and Nehemiah of the MT) is known as 3 Ezra in the Ethiopic enumeration.

laudable aim of removing the element of chance, of judgement based purely on impression, from the process of reconstruction, and within the limitations of his study he achieved a fair degree of success. But there are a number of methodological problems connected with his study, including not least the question of the extent to which the process of translation was a matter of instinct, not system. It is also of significance that he did not attempt at all to predict vocabulary.

The question of reconstruction is of some topicality in the Ethiopic sphere in view of the recently published edition by VanderKam and Milik of the Dead Sea fragments of the Hebrew text of the book of Jubilees.[1] The Book of Jubilees has survived in its entirety only in Ethiopic, but just over a quarter of the text has also been preserved in a sixth-century Latin palimpsest, and even after the discovery and publication of the Hebrew fragments the Ethiopic and the Latin versions still provide the major part of our knowledge of the text of this book. The Hebrew fragments are almost all quite small, but VanderKam and Milik have restored the text of many of the fragments quite extensively. The restorations are based primarily on the evidence of the Ethiopic and the Latin versions of Jubilees, and on the Hebrew text of Genesis and Exodus where this is relevant. There are methodological difficulties about the use of all three as a means of reconstructing the Hebrew text of Jubilees, but here I would like to comment specifically on the use made of the Ethiopic version.

The Ethiopic and the Latin versions of Jubilees are both daughter verions of the now lost Greek version of Jubilees, not of the original Hebrew text. There is every reason to think that the Ethiopic version provides us with a reasonably faithful translation of that lost Greek text — but subject to all the kinds of changes, made both at the time of the orignal translation and subsequently, that have been the concern of this lecture. There is a sufficient degree of consistency and

---

[1] J. VanderKam and J. T. Milik, 'Jubilees', in H. Attridge and others, *Qumran Cave 4.VIII: Parabiblical Texts, Part 1* (Discoveries in the Judaean Desert 13), Oxford, 1994, 1–140.

predictability about the Ethiopic version of the Old Testament to make it seem possible that one could reconstruct in broad terms what the Greek version of Jubilees would have been like, but — as I hope will have become apparent in this lecture — that is quite a different matter from being able to reconstruct that Greek text in detail. In the case of Jubilees, however, we are not trying to reconstruct the Greek, but rather the orignal Hebrew, and even though we have the fragments from Qumran on which to build, it will be apparent that the elements of uncertainty are considerably increased. The editors properly state in the edition: 'The Hebrew reconstructions ... merely retrovert the Ethiopic into Hebrew and are therefore tentative.'[1] The work has been done carefully, and it is no doubt interesting to see what the original Hebrew text of Jubilees might have looked like. But the publication of the Hebrew text of Jubilees restored on such an extensive scale in the official *Discoveries in the Judaean Desert* series gives the restored text an authority which it does not possess.

[1] VanderKam and Milik, *Qumran Cave 4.VIII*, 5.

Consistency and Diversity

I

Consistency of rendering is commonly regarded as a characteristic feature of a literal style of translation, although it is important to recognize that consistency and literalness are not the same thing.[1] Judged by the criterion of consistency, the Ethiopic Old Testament reveals some contradictory tendencies. Many Greek words are, it is true, always, or in a majority of cases, rendered by the same Ethiopic word,[2] but it is equally true that a variety of renderings for the same

[1] Cf. Barr, *The Typology of Literalism*, 31–33; Soisalon-Soininen, 'Methodologische Fragen der Erforschung der Septuaginta-Syntax', *Studien zur Septuaginta-Syntax*, 44–45. For a recent discussion of the limitations of using consistency as a measure of literality, see S. Olofsson, 'Consistency as a Translation Technique', *Scandinavian Journal of the Old Testament* 6 (1992), 14–30. For a somewhat different approach, see Tov and Wright, 'Computer-Assisted Study of the Criteria for Assessing the Literalness of Translation Units in the LXX', *Textus* 12 (1985), 149–87; Tov and Wright note that consistency and literalness are not the same, but use statistical techniques in an attempt to measure the degree of literality in different translation units of the Septuagint on the basis of the consistency in the use of certain renderings. Cf. Marquis, 'Consistency of Lexical Equivalents as a Criterion for the Evaluation of Translation Technique as Exemplified in the LXX of Ezekiel', in C. E. Cox (ed.), *VI Congress of the IOSCS*, 405–24.

[2] For some very pertinent comments on 'the tendency of the [Septuagint] translation to use constant equivalents', see Barr, 'Words for Love in Biblical Greek', in L. D. Hurst and N. T. Wright (eds), *The Glory of Christ in the New Testament: Studies in Christology in Memory of George Bradford Caird*, Oxford, 1987, 3–18, particularly 7–18.

Greek word can often be found. Sometimes these different renderings occur in close proximity to one another, and there seems no very obvious reason for this. My concern in this lecture is with the issues raised by this diversity of rendering, but before pursuing this I would like to make some comments of a more general nature concerning the treatment of the vocabulary of the Septuagint within the Ethiopic Bible, particularly concerning the adequacy of the renderings.

Study of any aspect of this subject is severely hampered by the lack of a Greek-Ethiopic concordance to the Ethiopic Old Testament — or even of a simple Ethiopic concordance. In a lecture given in Rome in 1972 the late Stefan Strelcyn listed the preparation of a critical editon of the entire Ethiopic Bible and the compilation of a concordance as being among the most urgent *desiderata* in Ethiopian studies,[1] but the continuing lack of reliable critical editions of all the books of the Ethiopic Old Testament makes the compilation of such a concordance as yet impossible. Valuable help is of course available from the numerous biblical references in Dillmann's *Lexicon*, and from the fact that Dillmann often gives the Greek words that lie behind the Ethiopic word he is discussing. But although the *Lexicon* contains an *Index Latinus*, there is no Greek index, and at present there are no short cuts for finding all the equivalents that are used in the Ethiopic Old Testament for, say, Greek διδόναι ('to give, to put') or for finding all the Greek words that are rendered by, say, Ethiopic ነበረ ('to sit'). Computer-assisted studies are likely in the future to be of assistance here, but in the current absence of reliable editions of all the books of the Ethiopic Old Testament from which a concordance might usefully be compiled, the present enquiry is based on a detailed study of the vocabulary of the Ethiopic Ezekiel and on soundings

---

[1] S. Strelcyn, 'Les manuscrits éthiopiens de quelques bibliothèques européens décrits récemment,' *IV Congresso Internazionale di Studi Etiopici* (Accademia Nazionale dei Lincei, Problemi attuali di scienza e di cultura, Quaderno N. 191), Rome, 1974, Tomo II, 61.

made in other parts of the Old Testament, particularly in the prophetic books.

II

It may be observed at the outset that in the majority of cases the words used in the Septuagint have been rendered perfectly adequately into Ethiopic, and it does appear that the translators had a reasonable grasp of Septuagint vocabulary, although this does not preclude the possibility of different levels of competence on the part of the translators of the different books. However, despite a general picture of semantic accuracy, there are numerous cases where incorrect or free renderings are found. We are not here concerned with the many cases where the lack of correspondence between the Greek and the Ethiopic word is the result of inner-Ethiopic development or of corruption within the Ethiopic text, but rather with those cases where the lack of correspondence goes back to the original translation. Nor are we concerned with cases of discrepancy between the Greek and the Ethiopic that derive from a misreading of the Greek text, or from corruption in the Greek text used by the translators. But apart from misreading or corruption, there were a number of other factors at the translation stage that affected the accuracy of the translation of the individual words.

As in the case of other ancient translations, one very obvious cause of incorrect renderings was failure to understand the original, but this can range from incompetence on a particular occasion to real lack of knowledge. In Ezek. 32:12 the Greek ἀπολοῦσι ('they will destroy') was wrongly taken by the translators to be from ἀπολούειν ('to wash off'), not from ἀπολλύειν/ἀπολλύναι.[1] A mistranslation of this kind hardly reflects well on the competence of the translators, and

[1] Ezek. 32:12: καὶ ἀπολοῦσι τὴν ὕβριν Αἰγύπτου, ወትትሐፀብ፡ ጽእለተ፡ ግብጽ፡ ('and the arrogance of Egypt will be washed off'); cf. Knibb, *JSS* 33 (1988), 25.

the assumption that the verb was the rare ἀπολούειν[1] and not the
common ἀπολλύειν is strange. But it is quite unlikely that the
misunderstanding occurred because the translator was unaware of the
meaning of the actual word used in the Greek. There are, however,
cases where this does seem likely. One such case occurs in Ezek.
16:5, where the Greek τῇ σκολιότητι τῆς ψυχῆς σου ('in the
crookedness of your life', that is 'in the perversity of your life') was
rendered by **ወተፀዕረት ፡ ነፍስኪ ፡** ('and your life was in torment').
σκολιότης is a rare word,[2] and in this instance it is plausible to think
that the translators were ignorant of the word they were translating
and simply guessed. But the difficulty in cases such as this is to know
with certainty whether we are dealing with an incorrect rendering that
is the result of ignorance, or with a free rendering, or indeed with a
rendering that is the outcome of the inner-Ethiopic development of the
text. We shall see this problem exemplified in other cases.

III

The adequacy of the Ethiopic translation of the Old Testament was
also materially affected by the fact that its vocabulary is considerably
restricted in comparison with that of the Septuagint, and the Ethiopic
does not reflect all the different words contained in the Septuagint
lexicon. It is perhaps hardly surprising that the numerous compounds
formed with prepositions such as ἀνά, ἀντί, ἀπό, διά, ἐκ and so on
are in the majority of cases translated in the same way as the simple
forms. But, as in the case of the Septuagint in relation to the Hebrew,
it is also true that many Ethiopic words have to do duty for a range of

---

[1] The verb only occurs in the Septuagint in Job 9:30, where it is properly rendered by
ኀፀበ ፡ III.1.

[2] The noun σκολιότης does not occur elsewhere in the Septuagint, but the adjective
σκολιός, for which the translation-equivalents **ዐለወ ፡** and **ጠዋይ ፡** are used, is not
infrequent.

Greek words in the same semantic field. Two examples from Ezekiel illustrate the range of equivalents that are found. ነገረ፡ ('to speak') is used eighteen times within Ezekiel as the equivalent of λαλεῖν ('to speak'),[1] but it is also used three times each as the equivalent of ἀπαγγέλλειν ('to announnce')[2] and λέγειν ('to say'),[3] and once each as the equivalent of ἀποφθέγγεσθαι ('to utter'), γνωρίζειν ('to make known'), δεικνύειν/δεικνύναι and παραδεικνύναι ('to show'), ἐκδιηγεῖσθαι ('to describe'), ἐλέγχειν ('to reprove'), and προαπαγγέλλειν ('to announce in advance, to warn');[4] and ምዕናር፡ ('dwelling') is used within Ezekiel once each as the equivalent of κατάλυμα and κατασκήνωσις (which both mean 'dwelling'), and of σκήνωμα ('tent'),[5] while the plural ምዕናር፡ is used once each as the equivalent of σκέπη (literally 'shelter, protection') and of ὅρμοι ('anchorage, harbour', and hence 'wall around the harbour').[6] The situation is complicated by the fact that for many Greek words more than one equivalent is used in the Ethiopic Old Testament, and this again mirrors the situation that obtains in the Septuagint. Thus, for example, three translation-equivalents are used in Ezekiel for λαλεῖν: ነበበ፡, which is used thirty-one times,[7] ነገረ፡, which, as we have seen, is used eighteen times,[8] and ተናገለ፡, which is used ten times.[9] (We

---

[1] 2:1, 7, 8; 3:4, 10, 18, 22; 11:25; 12:25bis, 28; 14:4; 20:3; 24:18; 29:3; 33:2, 30; 39:8.

[2] 23:36; 24:19; 37:18. B in all cases has ἀναγγέλλειν.

[3] 5:6; 17:2; 24:3; in the vast majority of cases ተናገለ፡ is used as the translation-equivalent for λέγειν.

[4] ἀποφθέγγεσθαι, 13:9; γνωρίζειν, 20:11; δεικνύειν/δεικνύναι, 40:4; παραδεικνύναι, 22:2; ἐκδιηγεῖσθαι, 12:16; ἐλέγχειν, (ነገረ፡ III.3, 3:26); προαπαγγέλλειν, 33:9.

[5] κατάλυμα, 23:21; κατασκήνωσις, 37:27; σκήνωμα, 25:4.

[6] σκέπη, 31:12; ὅρμοι, 27:11; for ὅρμοι, cf. J. Lust, E. Eynikel, and K. Hauspie, *A Greek-English Lexicon of the Septuagint*, 2 vols, Stuttgart, 1992, 1996, ii.339.

[7] 3:27; 5:13, 15, 17; 6:10; 10:5; 12:25, 28; 13:7; 14:9; 17:21, 24; 21:17, 32; 22:14, 28; 23:34; 24:14; 26:5, 14; 28:10; 30:12; 34:24; 36:5, 6, 36; 37:11, 14; 38:17, 19; 39:5.

[8] See above, n. 1.

shall see more examples of this kind later in this lecture.) However, the net effect is that the Ethiopic Old Testament deploys a smaller vocabulary than the Greek, and thus whereas the vocabulary of the Greek text of Ezekiel consists of approximately fifteen hundred words, the Ethiopic version uses approximately eleven hundred words.

Two consequences follow from this that should be noted here. First, the Ethiopic translation has a somewhat levelled-down appearance in comparison with the Septuagint because it is not able to reproduce the enormous variety of the Septuagint's vocabulary. And secondly, accurate prediction of the vocabulary of the Septuagint on the basis of the vocabulary used in the Ethiopic would clearly not be possible.

IV

Inasmuch as the renderings that are used are not actually wrong, they fall somewhere on a scale that runs from the literal to the extremely free. At one end of the scale, the separate translation of the two halves of Greek compounds, that is segmentation below the level of the word, represents an extreme of literality.[1] Translations of this kind occur quite frequently in Ezekiel where, for example, ἀλλογενής is

---

[9] 2:1, 2; 3:1, 11, 24; 12:23; 20:27; 33:8, 10, 30. (24:27; 43:6; 44:5 are not represented in the older type of text.)

[1] Barr (*The Typology of Literalism*, 36–40), dealing with the related issue of consistency, surveys 'the various possible positions on the scale between free and literal in respect of constancy in the use of equivalents.' — For segmentation below word level in the Greek translations of the Old Testament, see Barr, *The Typology of Literalism*, 26–29. However, segmentation below word level functions differently in the Ethiopic translation from the way it does in the Greek. Thus whereas there are many compounds in Greek whose component parts can be analysed separately, Hebrew words — with the exception of many proper names — cannot, as Barr reminds us, be split into component morphemes.

rendered by ዘእምባዕድ፡ ዘመድ፡ ('of another race', Ezek. 44:9) and ἀλλόγλωσσος by እለ፡ ካልእ፡ ልሳኖሙ፡ ('whose tongue is different', Ezek. 3:6). Comparable expressions are used for many other compounds such as those formed with βαθυ- ('deep'), βαρυ- ('heavy'), μεγα- ('great'), σκληρο- ('hard') and are normally quite straightforward. But literalism of this kind can produce some curious results. ἀποσφράγμισμα ('seal, signet ring') occurs twice in the Old Testament, and in Jer. 22:24 it is properly rendered into Ethiopic as 'signet ring' (ሕልቀት፡ ማዕተብ፡ or just ማዕተብ፡).[1] But in Ezek. 28:12 it is rendered by ፍቱሕ፡ ማሕተም፡ , literally 'loosed of a signet', which is almost unintelligible — except that ፍቱሕ፡ 'loosed' is probably to be explained as an attempt to give separate expression to the prefix ἀπο-, as Cornill long ago suggested.[2]

Transliteration, from Greek to Ethiopic and from Hebrew to Ethiopic, represents another type of literality,[3] but it is difficult to know in such cases whether the achievement of literality was consciously intended; in many cases, I would suggest, this was not the intention. Within Ezekiel it is perhaps surprising to observe that some sixty words out of a total vocabulary of approximately fifteen hundred words were transliterated from Greek into Ethiopic, although it should be noted that many of these are technical terms, and that they are to be found particularly in the foreign nation oracles (chapters 25–32) and

---

[1] The former occurs in Berlin Peterm. II, Nachtr. 42 (15th cent.), the latter in EMML 2080 (15th/16th cent.).

[2] Cornill, *Ezechiel*, 40–41.

[3] For transliteration in the Greek Bible, see H. St John Thackeray, *A Grammar of the Old Testament in Greek according to the Septuagint*, vol. I: *Introduction, Orthography and Accidence*, Cambridge, 1909, 31–38; Tov, 'Transliterations of Hebrew Words in the Greek Versions of the Old Testament: A Further Characteristic of the *kaige*-Th. Revision?', *Textus* 8 (1973), 78–92; id., 'Did the Septuagint Translators always Understand their Hebrew Text?', in A. Pietersma and C. Cox (eds), *De Septuaginta: Studies in Honour of John William Wevers on his Sixty-fifth Birthday*, Mississauga, Ontario, 1984, 55–56.

in the description of the restored temple (chapters 40–48). In some
cases the transliterations are merely an indication of the carelessness
of the translator, as for example the transliteration of the formulaic
expression in Ezek. 48:1 Δαν, μία ('Dan, one portion') by ደንሞያ ፡ ,
as if it were the name of a country;[1] or the transliteration of the
negative οὐδ' in Ezek. 16:28 by ሑዶ ፡ as if it were a proper name like
Ασσουρ.[2] But more often than not transliteration from the Greek
seems to be another example of what has been described by Barr as an
'easy technique'.[3] It is certainly in this light that I would view the
transliteration into Ethiopic of those words that had already been
transliterated from Hebrew into Greek, such as αβαμα (Hebrew הבמה,
'high place'; Ezek. 20:29),[4] or αιλαμ (Hebrew אולם, אילם 'vestibule');[5]
or the words expressing the directions 'east' (κεδεμ) and 'south'
(δαρωμ, θαιμαν and ναγεβ);[6] or the words for precious stones,
λαμωθ and κορκορ (Hebrew ראמת and כדכד, perhaps 'corals' and
'rubies'; Ezek. 27:16).[7] I would also regard the transliteration of the
various Greek technical terms that are found in Ezekiel as further

---

[1] In Ezek. 48:2–7, 23–27 the formula was reproduced correctly, e.g. v. 2: Ασηρ, μία,
ኣሴር ፡ ኣሐቲ ፡ .

[2] Ezek. 16:28: ἐπὶ τὰς θυγατέρας Ασσουρ καὶ οὐδ', ምስለ ፡ ኣዋልደ ፡ ኣሱር ፡ ወሑዶ ፡ .

[3] Cf. Barr, *The Typology of Literalism*, 26, 50.

[4] Ezek. 20:29: הבמה, αβαμα (var. βαμα), ባማ ፡ . However, αβαμα was perhaps understood
as a proper name in the Greek.

[5] See e.g. Ezek. 8:16: האולם, τῶν αιλαμ, ኤላም ፡ . For αιλαμ/ኤላም ፡ , see also above, p. 38;
the term is used very frequently in Ezek. 40–46, particularly in chapters 40 and 41.

[6] See Ezek: 25:4, 10: קדם, κεδεμ, ቄዶም ፡ (so also in Jer. 30:6 (MT 49:28)); Ezek. 20:46
(MT 21:2): נגב ... דרום ... תימנה, θαιμαν ... δαρωμ (var. δαρωρ) ... ναγεβ, ቴማን ፡ ... ጻሮም ፡ ...
ናጌብ ፡ . However, all four words appear to have been understood in the Greek as proper
nouns, and ναγεβ/ናጌብ ፡ for נגב also occurs in Ezek. 20:47 (MT 21:3) and elsewhere, e.g.
Jer. 39:44 (MT 32:44).

[7] Ezek. 27:16: וראמת וכדכד, καὶ ραμωθ (var. λαμωθ) καὶ χορχορ (var. κορχορ), ወላሞት ፡
ወቆርኮር ፡ .

examples of an 'easy technique'.¹ These technical terms include a
substantial number of names of precious stones, such as — in the list
in Ezek. 28:13 — ἀμέθυστος and ἀχάτης;² names of trees, such as
ἐλάται ('firs'; Ezek. 31:8);³ architectural terms, such as γεῖσος
('cornice'; Ezek. 40:43),⁴ ἐξέδρα ('chamber'),⁵ and ἐπωμίδες ('side-
walls');⁶ and a miscellaneous group consisting of words such as αὖρα

---

¹ Cf. Conti Rossini, *Storia d'Etiopia*, 224: 'Quando poi si trova di fronte a termini
tecnici, a nomi di piante, a voci d'origine forestiera, a vocaboli difficili o men conosciuti,
il traduttore spesso si limita a trascriverli semplicemente in lettere etiopiche e ad inserirli
nella lor forma graeca, senz'altro, nella sua versione.'

² Ezek. 28:13: καὶ ἀχάτην καὶ ἀμέθυστον, ወአኪጤን ፡ ወአሜተስሞን ፡ .

³ Ezek. 31:8: καὶ ἐλάται, ወኢላጢ ፡ . In Gen. 21:15 ἐλάτη is rendered by the word for
'tree' (ዕፅ ፡), and in Song of Solomon 5:11 βόστρυχοι αὐτοῦ ἐλάται is rendered as
ፀምፀሙሁ ፡ ፅሉል ፡ ('his hair is curly').

⁴ Ezek. 40:43: γεῖσος, ጊሡም ፡ . γεῖσος is not represented elsewhere in the older Ethiopic
text of Ezekiel, nor in the Old Ethiopic of Jer. 52:22, but in 3 Kingdoms 7:46 (MT 7:9) it
is rendered by ጣፈር ፡ ('roof').

⁵ See e.g Ezek. 40:45: ἐξέδρα, ኢክስድራ ፡ ; 40:44: ἐξέδραι, ኢክስድራ ፡ ; 41:10: ἐξεδρῶν,
ኢክስድርን ፡ .

⁶ See Ezek. 40:48; 41:2: ἐπωμίδες, ኤጶሚዶስ ፡ ; 41:3: τὰς ἐπωμίδας, ኤጶሚዳስ ፡ . ἐπωμίδες
is used as the equivalent of מזוזה in 41:2, but the Hebrew word does not occur in the
other two passages. ἐπωμίς also occurs in Exod. 28:7; 36:11 (MT 39:4) as the equivalent
of כתף (with the meaning 'shoulder-piece') and frequently in Exod. 25–36 (MT 25–39)
and some other passages as the stereotyped equivalent of אפד. In Exod. 28:7 ἐπωμίδες is
transliterated as ኤጶዱሞስ ፡ (or a similar form), but in Exod. 36:11 ἐπωμίδας is
translated as ልብሰ ፡ መትከፍት ፡ (literally 'garment of the shoulder'). In Exod. 25:6 (MT
25:7) εἰς τὴν ἐπωμίδα καὶ τὸν ποδήρη is transliterated as ኤጶሚጶደሮር ፡ , but otherwise a
variety of translations is used for ἐπωμίς (= אפד), e.g. ትብልያ ፡ ዘመቅፈርት ፡ (Exod. 28:4),
ትብልያ ፡ (Exod. 28:6, 8), መልበስት ፡ (Exod. 28:15, 25), and ዐጽፍ ፡ (Exod. 35:8 (MT 9),
27).

('aura'; Ezek. 8:2)[1] or παραλία (sea-coast'; Ezek. 25:16).[2] The list of precious stones — twelve according to the Old Greek and the Ethiopic — in Ezek. 28:13 has been borrowed from the list of the precious stones on the breastpiece of the high priest in Exod. 28:17–20 (cf. 36:17–20 (MT 39:10–13)), and in the Ethiopic version of Exodus the Greek names have likewise been transliterated, although with some differences from the forms used in Ezekiel.[3]

If it is right to think that transliteration seemed to the translators the easy and natural way to handle both words that had been transliterated from Hebrew into Greek and Greek technical terms, it is nonetheless curious that some words were transliterated in one passage and translated in another. For example, the Greek word ἀρά ('vow, oath') occurs twice in Ezekiel; in 17:16 it is translated quite properly by መሐላ ፥ , but three verses earlier it is transliterated by ኣራ ፥ ; in fact the word seems to have been taken as a proper name in that the formula 'and he will make him enter into an oath' (καὶ εἰσάξει αὐτὸν ἐν ἀρᾷ) has been mistranslated as 'and he will lead him into Ara' (ወያወስዶ ፥ ውስተ ፥ ኣራ ፥). To take another example, γωνία ('corner') is twice translated quite normally in Ezekiel by ማእዝን ፥ (43:20; 45:19), but in 41:15 — in an admittedly obscure context —

---

[1] Ezek. 8:2: αὔρας (=זהר), አውራስ ፥ . Elsewhere αὔρα is used as the equvalent of ממד; in Ps. 106:29 (MT 107:29) the text is paraphrased, in 3 Kingdoms 19:12 αὔρα is rendered by ፉጻፀ ፥ III.3 ('to whistle, hiss'), and in Job 4:16 by ጽላሎት ፥ ('shadow').

[2] Ezek. 25:16: τὴν παραλίαν, ኣራልያ ፥ . So elsewhere, e.g. Isa. 9:1 (MT 8:23).

[3] Brock ('Aspects of Translation Technique in Antiquity', 84–85) notes that for technical terms three possibilities were open: 'transcription, etymological translation (usually a neologism) or cultural equivalent', and it is sometimes the case that technical terms were translated in the Ethiopic Bible. Cf. Ezek. 4:2: καὶ οἰκοδομήσεις ἐπ' αὐτὴν προμαχῶνας, ወተሕንጽ ፥ ውስቴታ ፥ ኀበ ፥ ይትቃተሉ ፥ (literally 'and you shall build against it where they fight one another'). προμαχών is translated in the same way in Jer. 5:10; 40:4 (MT 33:4); cf. Schäfers, *Die äthiopische Übersetzung des Propheten Jeremias*, 73-74. But in Tob. 13:17 προμαχῶνες is rendered by ኣናቅጽ ፥ ('gates').

the plural αἱ γωνίαι is transliterated by አጓኔዉ : .[1] Again, λειοπετρία ('smooth, bare rock') is, for no very obvious reason, twice translated in Ezekiel (26:4, 14)[2] and twice transliterated (24:7, 8)[3] It may be argued that in cases like these transliteration may either reflect incompetence on the part of the translator (so in the case of ἀρά, or of μία and οὐδ' discussed above), or be the outcome of a purely arbitrary procedure (so in the case of λειοπετρία), or, exceptionally, represent a conscious attempt to preserve the exact form of a text which, for whatever reason, was not properly understood (so, I would suggest, in the case of αἱ γωνίαι). However, with regard to the main bulk of the transliterations from or via the Greek, we appear to have to do with the use of an 'easy technique', and in these cases it may be wondered how far there was a proper understanding of the meaning of the transliterated words.

Transliterations from the Hebrew were discussed in the first lecture, and they have been, as we noted, the object of a special study by Professor Edward Ullendorff. I do not wish to add to what I said in the first lecture other than to repeat that in my view transliterations from the Hebrew belong to the latest layer in the development of the Ethiopic text, but that in that layer they represent a very significant element indeed.[4]

---

[1] Ezek. 41:15: καὶ ὁ ναὸς καὶ αἱ γωνίαι καὶ τὸ αιλαμ τὸ ἐξώτερον πεφατνωμένα, ወጽርሑኂ : ወአጓኔዉ : ወኢላም : ጸናፈ : መናብርት : ('And the temple, and 'the corners', and the outer vestibule, the thresholds' (?)).

[2] Ezek. 26:4: καὶ δώσω αὐτὴν εἰς λειοπετρίαν, ወአሪስያ : ከመ : ኰኵሕ : ልሙጽ : ; Ezek. 26:14: καὶ δώσω σε εἰς λειοπετρίαν, ወአረስየኪ : ከመ : ኰኵሕ : ንጹሕ : .

[3] Ezek. 24:7, 8: ἐπὶ λειοπετρίαν, ዲበ : ሊዮጼጥርያ : .

[4] See above, pp. 35–40.

V

Free renderings occur very frequently in the Ethiopic Old Testament, but it is often difficult to determine whether a particular translation should be so regarded in that free renderings can range from being a good interpretation of the original to being incorrect. The difficulties are illustrated by a number of cases that occur in the Old Ethiopic text of Daniel 1. In verse 7 the Greek 'the chief of the eunuchs assigned (ἐπέθηκεν) names to them' has been translated as 'the chief of the eunuchs changed (ወለጠሙ፡) their names'. In this context ወለጠ፡ ('change') is a good idiomatic rendering of ἐπιτιθέναι ('assign'), and in fact the same equivalent is used in a similar context in 4 Kingdoms 24:17.[1] In Dan. 1:10 the Greek σκυθρωπός ('dejected, downcast') has been rendered by ድጉዓግ፡ ('emaciated, thin'), which occurs as the equivalent of λεπτός in Gen. 41:3–4. The literal equivalent of σκυθρωπός is ሕዙን፡ , which is used in a comparable context in Gen. 40:7. But 'emaciated' suits the context of Dan. 1:10 very well, and ድጉዓግ፡ may be regarded as a reasonable interpretation of the Greek word.[2] In Dan. 1:8 Daniel resolves, according to the Greek, not to be polluted (ἀλισγηθῇ) by the food and wine provided by Nebuchadnezzar, but according to the Ethiopic he resolves not to eat (በልዐ፡) or drink (ሰትየ፡) the food or wine.[3] In a case such as this it is difficult to know whether the translator was unaware of the meaning of the Greek word, or whether free translation has been taken to an extreme. In practice in this particular instance it is the latter that seems most likely. The whole passage is treated with considerable

---

[1] Dan. 1:7: καὶ ἐπέθηκεν αὐτοῖς ὁ ἀρχιευνοῦχος ὀνόματα, ወወለጠሙ፡ አስማቲሆሙ፡ ለቀ፡ ገጽዎን፡ ; 4 Kingdoms 24:17: καὶ ἐπέθηκεν τὸ ὄνομα αὐτοῦ Σεδεκια, ወወለጠ፡ ስሞ፡ ሴዴቅያስ፡ ሰመየ፡ .

[2] Dan. 1:10: μήποτε ἴδῃ τὰ πρόσωπα ὑμῶν σκυθρωπά, ከመ፡ ርእየከሙ፡ ድጉዓጋኒከሙ፡ ; Gen. 40:7: Τί ὅτι τὰ πρόσωπα ὑμῶν σκυθρωπά;, ምንትኑ፡ ሕዙናን፡ ገጽከሙ፡ .

[3] Dan. 1:8: ὡς οὐ μὴ ἀλισγηθῇ ἐν τῇ τραπέζῃ τοῦ βασιλέως καὶ εὐ τῷ οἴνῳ τοῦ πότου αὐτοῦ, ከመ፡ ኢይብላዕ፡ እማእደ፡ ንጉሥ፡ ወከመ፡ ኢይስተይ፡ እምወይኑ፡ .

freedom, and although ἀλισγεῖν ('to pollute') is not a common word, it is rendered literally in the four cases where it occurs in Malachi 1.[1]

As another example of the difficulties of drawing a line between a rendering that is free and one that is incorrect, reference may be made to Ezek. 16:4, where the Greek σπαργάνοις οὐκ ἐσπαργανώθης ('you were not wrapped in swaddling-clothes') has been rendered by ው·ስት ፡ ሕፅን ፡ ኢ.ሐፀኑ·ኪ. ፡ ('you were not nursed in the bosom'). σπάργανον ('swaddling-clothes') and σπαργανοῦν ('to wrap in swaddling-clothes') are rare words and are both used only once each elsewhere in the Septuagint. But in Wisdom 7:4 the noun is rendered literally by ኅፅርፇት ፡ and in Job 38:9 the verb is rendered literally by ጠብለለ ፡ , and it is not clear why these words were not used in Ezekiel. Thus it is not clear whether, through ignorance, the translator was forced to guess at the meaning of σπάργανον and σπαργανοῦν, or whether he deliberately chose a very free rendering that is in effect a mistranslation.

Two particular kinds of free rendering deserve separate mention. On the one hand it sometimes happens that words with a quite specific meaning in Greek have been rendered by a word with a very general meaning in Ethiopic. Thus, for example, in Ezek. 2:6 παροιστρᾶν ('to sting, sting to madness') has been rendered by the general term ርፅ ፡ ('to assail, attack').[2] Similarly ፀር ፡ ('enemy, adversary') has to serve for βάρβαρος ('barbarous, foreign', Ezek. 21:31 (MT 21:36)),[3] አልባስ ፡ ('clothes') for τιάραι ('head-dresses',

---

[1] The three occurrences of the perfect participle passive ἠλισγημένος are rendered by the adjectives ርኩስ ፡ ('unclean'; Mal. 1:7) and ጐዋር ፡ ('polluted'; Mal. 1:7, 12), the aorist ἠλισγήσαμεν by ረኩስ ፡ II.1 ('to make unclean'; Mal. 1:7).

[2] In Hos. 4:16 παροιστρᾶν is used intransitively: ὡς δάμαλις παροιστρῶσα παροίστρησεν Ισραηλ. The Old Ethiopic has ከመ ፡ ኮ·ልት ፡ አንት ፡ ተሰክበ ፡ ሰበ ፡ አስራኤል ፡ ('as a heifer lies down, Israel lies down') and appears to have taken the verb to be παραστρωννύναι. Other manscripts, with a later text, have ዐብረየ ፡ ('to be mad').

[3] So also in Ps. 113:1 (MT 114:1).

Ezek. 23:15),[1] and አኩይ፥ ('evil') for φιλόνεικος ('contentious', Ezek. 3:7). The use of renderings of this kind is perhaps partly to be explained by the fact that the lexical resources available to the translators were limited, as we noted earlier; but this is only part of the explanation, and sometimes the use of renderings of this kind appears to be little more than the result of casualness. In Ezek. 16:22 πεφυρμένη ('wallowing'), from the comparatively rare verb φύρεσθαι, is rendered perfectly adequately by ዐንቀቀ፥ which likewise means 'wallowing', but in 16:6 the same form is rendered by the common verb ስክብ፥ ('to lie') for no very obvious reason.[2] Again, in Dan. 2:5 there seems no obvious reason why ንዋይ፥ (here probably to be understood as 'property, possessions'), and not the regular translation-equivalent ቤት፥ , should be used for οἱ οἶκοι ὑμῶν ('your houses'). However, whatever their origin, renderings of this generalising type do not adequately reflect the meaning of the underlying Greek words.

In contrast to the above, there are cases where the Ethiopic uses a word with a more precise meaning than the Greek word. In part this may be understood as translating according to the sense, and renderings of this kind are, not surprisingly, particularly to be found in the case of words like διδόναι ('to give, to put') which, like the underlying Hebrew verb נתן, has a very wide range of meanings. Thus while ወሀብ፥ ('to give') and ረሰይ፥ ('to put') are the two most common translation-equivalents of διδόναι, nearly forty other renderings can be found within Ezekiel, for example አርአይ፥ ('to show', 3:20), አውረደ፥ ('to cast down', 13:11), ሴሰየ፥ ('to feed', 16:19). To mention some other examples, in Ezek. 5:1 the prophet is told to 'shave'

---

[1] τιάραι is not represented in the Old Ethiopic version of Dan. 3:21.

[2] Ezek. 16:22: καὶ πεφυρμένη ἐν τῷ αἵματί σου ἔζησας, ወዐንቀቀት፥ አንቲ፥ በደምኪ፥ ሕየኪ፥ ; Ezek. 16:6: καὶ εἶδόν σε πεφυρμένην ἐν τῷ αἵματι σου, ወርኢኩኪ፥ ትስብሊ፥ ውስተ፥ ደምኪ፥ . ስክብ፥ is also used in 2 Kingdoms 20:12, but elsewhere a variety of renderings is ued for φύρεσθαι, e.g. በትብት፥ ('to decay, become putrid'; Job 7:5), ኡስ፥ ('to waste away, languish'; Job 30:14), መልአ፥ ('to be full'; Isa. 14:19).

(ተላፀየ ፡) his head with the sword rather than merely to 'run the sword over' (ἐπάγειν) his head; in 10:15 the cherubim are said to 'fly up' (ሰረረ ፡) rather than to 'rise up' (ἐπαίρειν); and in 15:4 the wood which is burnt is said to 'become ashes' (ሐመደ ፡) rather than to 'cease to exist' (ἐκλείπειν). In all such cases as these the Ethiopic word is appropriate to the context, but there remains a problem in that it is difficult to be certain that renderings such as these do go back to the original translation and are not rather the outcome of the internal development of the Ethiopic text or of direct influence from a Syro-Arabic text. In the first lecture we noticed a number of cases where influence from the Syro-Arabic version on the vocabulary of the Ethiopic version could clearly be detected, and I may mention just one further example here. In Ezek. 9:10 the Greek 'I bring their ways on their heads' (τὰς ὁδοὺς αὐτῶν εἰς κεφαλὰς αὐτῶν δέδωκα) has become 'I will repay them according to their ways on their heads' (እፈድዮሙ ፡ በከመ ፡ ፍኖቶሙ ፡ ዲበ ፡ ርእሶሙ ፡). The use of ፈደየ ፡ ('to repay, reward, requite') as the equivalent for διδόναι is entirely appropriate to the context and might be attributed to the translator. But in the other three passages in Ezekiel where this formula occurs (11:21; 16:43; 22:31) the Ethiopic uses ገብአ ፡ II.1 ('to give back, return'),[1] and this verb is in any case used quite frequently as a translation-equivalent for διδόναι. The Syro-Arabic version of Ezek. 9:10 has a construction with جزاء جزى (literally 'to give back a reward, give back requital'), and it seems more likely that the occurrence of ፈደየ ፡ rather than ገብአ ፡ II.1 in this passage reflects influence from the Syro-Arabic version than that it goes back to the original translator.

Free renderings of the kind that I have been discussing can be found very frequently in all parts of the Ethiopic Old Testament, and they clearly have a material effect on the semantic accuracy of the translation. Detailed study on the basis of reliable texts is, however, required to determine whether such free renderings occur more

---

[1] Cf. e.g. Ezek. 11:21: τὰς ὁδοὺς αὐτῶν εἰς κεφαλὰς αὐτῶν δέδωκα, ፍኖቲሆሙ ፡ ዲበ ፡ ርእሶሙ ፡ አግባእኩ ፡ ሎሙ ፡ .

frequently in certain parts of the Old Testament, for example the prophetic books, than in others.

VI

In the course of this lecture we have already had occasion to notice that the Ethiopic is not always consistent in its rendering of individual words, and I would now like to turn specifically to the question of consistency and inconsistency. It is of course true that for very many words the Ethiopic version always, or almost always, uses the same rendering for a particular Greek word,[1] and this can be illustrated by some statistics from the translation of Ezekiel. Within the Old Greek translation of Ezekiel there are approximately two hundred and thirty verbs, nouns and adjectives that occur ten times or more. Of these, some seventy words are always translated by the same Ethiopic word or use related verbal and nominal forms from the same Ethiopic root.[2] For some sixty Greek words, two Ethiopic words or roots are used, but for two thirds of these one word or root is clearly dominant, and it is only in one or two exceptional cases that a different rendering is used.[3] Much the same applies for the remaining one hundred or so

[1] For stereotyped renderiings in the Greeek Bible, see e.g. Tov, 'Three Dimensions of LXX Words', *RB* 83 (1976), 532–40; J. A. L. Lee, 'Equivocal and Stereoptyped Renderings in the LXX, *RB* 87 (1980), 111–17; Barr, *The Typology of Literalism*, 36–37.

[2] In many cases this was simply because the Ethiopic word was the obvious, if not the only, word to use (cf. Barr, *The Typology of Literalism*, 32), as in the following examples: ἐπιγινώσκειν — አአሞረ : , λέων — ዐንበሳ : , λίμος — ረኃብ : , μιμνῄσκεσθαι — ዘከረ : , παραπικραίνειν — መረረ : or መሰረ : .

[3] Cf. the following examples in Ezekiel (in each case the standard equivalent is given first):

αἰχμαλωσία — ፄዋ : or ፄወወ :] ወሰደ : ('to lead away', 12:11)

βραχίων — መዝራዕት :] ኵርናዕ : ('elbow, forearm', 13:20)

ἐγγίζειν — ቀርበ :] አልጸቀ : (9:1; 12:23)

Greek words, for which three or more Ethiopic words or roots are used. In the case of half of these one word or root is dominant, and exceptions are confined to one or two cases.[1] Thus approximately one hundred and sixty of the two hundred and thirty verbs, nouns and adjectives that occur ten times or more in Ezekiel always, or almost always, have the same translation equivalent, or use forms from the same root. And even for those Greek words where the picture is less clear cut, it is usually the case that one rendering is used more than the others and approaches being the standard equivalent.

The overall picture that emerges from an analysis of the words used ten times or more in the Old Greek version of Ezekiel is confirmed by an analysis of the words used less than ten times, and well over half of all the words used in the Greek Ezekiel are always rendered by the same Ethiopic word or by forms from a single root. A

ἐκδίκησις — በቀλ፡ or በቀλ፡] መቅሠፍት፡ ('blow, torment, (divine) punishment', 5:15; 9:1; 14:21)

καταβαίνειν — ወረደ፡] ደድፈ፡ ('to fall down', 30:6)

The reason for the employment of such non-standard equivalents needs to be examined on a case-by-case basis, and it cannot automatically be assumed that the non-standard equivalent was used in the original translation.

[1] Cf. the following examples in Ezekiel (in each case the standard equivalent is given first):

ἀκούειν — ሰምዐ፡] አዕምኸ፡ (12:2; 33:31; 40:4), አእመረ፡ ('to understand', 3:6)

δόξα — ስብሐት፡] ክብር፡ (39:21), ትርሲት፡ (27:7, 10)

ἐξέρχεσθαι — ወፅአ፡] ሐረ፡ ('to go', 3:22, 23), ሰምዐ፡ III.1 ('to be heard, be spread (of fame)', 16:14); also ሐበረ፡ II.1 ('to clean off', 24:6), ነሥአ፡ ፡ II.1 ('to raise', 21:4)

ὄρος — ደብር፡] ደወλ፡ ('region', but frequently used for ὄρος, ὄρη, 28:14; 37:22), ብሔር፡ ('land', 39:2)

πίπτειν — ወድቀ፡] መጽአ፡ ('to come', 11:5), በጽሐ፡ ('to befall', 24:6), ሞተ፡ ('to die', 17:21), ነዐ፡ III.1 ('to be thrown down, to fall to the ground', 29:5)

The comment made at the end of the preceding note applies all the more in cases like these.

sampling of the evidence in other books of the Ethiopic Old Testament indicates that there was a similar consistency of rendering throughout the translation and confirms the use of the same translation-equivalents. But this is an area where there needs to be detailed study of individual books of the Old Testament to see whether there is any significant variation in the degree of consistency and — if there is variation — whether this is linked to the age of the manuscripts that are available. There is no Ethiopic manuscript of Ezekiel available that is earlier than the fifteenth century, and it needs to be asked whether a book for which older manuscripts, and an older type of text, are available shows a greater or lesser degree of consistency.

As we noted above, the use of stereotyped renderings is regarded as one of the features of a literal style of translation,[1] but again it has to be asked how far the achievement of literalness was the intention of the translators. As Barr and Aejmalaeus have emphasised in relation to the Septuagint, stereotyped renderings are used because in the vast majority of cases they fit naturally into the context, and their use represents an 'easy' technique.[2] Barr has suggested that consistency of rendering in the Septuagint may have been encouraged by the use by the translators of primitive word-lists,[3] and there is a sufficient degree of consistency in the Ethiopic version to make such a suggestion plausible here also. But the use of standard equivalents as a matter of convenience, whether or not in conjuction with the use of word-lists, is quite a different thing from a conscious attempt to acheive absolute consistency — and there is more than enough evidence to make it quite unlikely that the translators had such an intention.

---

[1] See above, p. 87, n. 1.

[2] Cf. Barr, *The Typology of Literalism*, 36–37, 50; Aejmelaeus, 'Translation Technique and the Intention of the Translator', *On the Trail*, 67–72, 75–76.

[3] See preceding note.

VII

Over against the picture of consistency that has just been described, there is also widespread evidence of diversity of rendering. A very good illustration of this is to be found in the renderings used in the Old Ethiopic text of Daniel 2 for three Greek verbs that are used repeatedly in the narrative. ἀναγγέλλειν ('to announce, to declare') is used eleven times in Dan. 2 and is rendered ten times by ነገረ : ('to tell') and once by አይድዐ : ('to make known').[1] ἀποκαλύπτειν ('to reveal') is used seven times in Dan. 2 and is rendered five times by ከሠተ : , which has exactly the same meaning as the Geek word, once by ርእየ : ('to see'), where we expect rather አርአየ : ('to show'), and once by አለመረ : ('to indicate').[2] Thus for these two verbs the degree of consistency corresponds to what we have seen in Ezekiel. By contrast, for γνωρίζειν ('to make known'), which occurs eleven times in Dan. 2, four different renderings are used: ነገረ : ('to tell') on four occasions, አይድዐ : ('to make known'), and አርአየ : ('to show') three times each, and አለመረ : ('to indicate') once.[3] γνωρίζειν is used in exactly the same way throughout Daniel 2, and there is nothing in the Greek text which would provide a reason for this complete diversity of rendering in the Ethiopic.

The incidence of lack of consistency is to some extent related to the size of the semantic field to which a word, or group of words, belongs. To take a simple example, in principle a distinction can be drawn between Greek θύρα ('door', Hebrew פתח or דלת) and πύλη ('gate', Hebrew שער). In his *Lexicon* Dillmann notes that at one stage a similar distinction was apparently made in Ethiopic between ኆኅት :

---

[1] ἀναγγέλλειν] ነገረ : : Dan. 2:2, 7, 9bis, 11, 16, 24, 25, 26, 27; አይድዐ : : Dan. 2:4.

[2] ἀποκαλύπτειν] ከሠተ : : Dan. 2:19, 22, 28, 29, 30; ርእየ : [አርአየ :]: Dan. 2:47; አለመረ : : Dan. 2:47. (In both v. 47 and in v. 10 [see next note] the text has the infinitive አለምሮ : ; for the form, see Löfgren, *Daniel*, 103; Dillmann, *Lexicon*, col. 730.)

[3] γνωρίζειν] ነገረ : : Dan. 2:15, 17, 23, 30; አይድዐ : : Dan. 2:5, 6, 23; አርአየ : : Dan. 2:28, 29, 45; አለመረ : : Dan. 2:10.

('door') and አንቀጽ ፡ ('gate'), but that in many passages the words are used promiscuously.[1] The situation is complicated by the fact that in Ethiopic two other words are also used for θύρα, πύλη and related words, namely ዩዩ ፡ ('gate, entrance') and ማዕጾ ፡ ('door'). Thus within Ezekiel, whereas ኆኅት ፡ is almost invariably used as the translation equivalent for θύρα, ማዕጾ ፡ is also used once (38:11); and whereas አንቀጽ ፡ is used thirty-five times as the translation equivalent of πύλη, ኆኅት ፡ is used twenty-seven times and ዩዩ ፡ fourteen times. The lack of consistency in regard to πύλη is particular evident in Ezekiel 40 where the forty-four occurrences of this word are divided up among the three Ethiopic words in the ratio 16:12:10 (plus six omissions).[2] A similar diversity of rendering is also apparent if other words in this field are included, such as θύρωμα ('doorway, door'),[3] πυλών ('gateway'),[4] and πρόθυρον ('porch, portico').[5]

To take an example from a theological field, it is to be observed that within Ezekiel Ethiopic ኃጢአት ፡ ('sin') is the predominat translation equivalent for ἀδικία ('wrongdoing'), ἁμαρτία ('sin'), ἀνομία ('transgression') and ἀσέβεια ('impiety'), but that for all four words other equivalents are used indiscriminately, particularly ጌጋይ ፡ ('crime'), ዐመጻ ፡ ('iniquity'), and አበሳ ፡ ('wrongdoing').[6] *Mutatis*

---

[1] Dillmann, *Lexicon*, col. 606: quamvis [ኆኅት ፡] primitus ab አንቀጽ ፡ ita distinctum esse videatur, ut פתח a שער, tamen multis in locis ኆኅት ፡ et አንቀጽ ፡ promiscue usurpantur.

[2] አንቀጽ ፡ : 40:3, 6bis, 9bis, 13bis, 15, 20 (πύλη variant for αὐλῆ), 22, 23bis, 32, 35, 38, 44; ኆኅት ፡ : 40:10, 13, 14, 19bis, 27quater, 40, 41, 44; ዩዩ ፡ : 40:15, 16, 18bis, 20, 23tris, 28, 39; omissions: 40:9, 14, 15, 21, 24, 28.

[3] θύρωμα] ኆኅት ፡ : 40:38; 41:3tris, 22, 23; አንቀጽ ፡ : 40:48; ማዕጾ ፡ : 41:24.

[4] πυλών] ኆኅት ፡ : 40:9 (Ethiopic plural); 41:2; አንቀጽ ፡ : 40:11bis; ዩዩ ፡ : 33:30; 41:2.

[5] πρόθυρον] መድርክ ፡ (literally 'threshold'): 46:3a; πρόθυρα] ኆኅት ፡ : 8:7, 16; 11:1; አንቀጽ ፡ : 8:14; 10:19. (The Ethiopic differs in 46:2, 3b and does not have the passage in 43:8; 47:1.)

[6] Compare the following examples: ἀδικία/ἀδικίαι] ኃጢአት ፡ : 3:18; 4:4bis; 18:19, 20; ጌጋይ ፡ : 3:19; 4:5; 18:18; ዐመጻ ፡ : 9:9; 18:17; 28:18; አበሳ ፡ : 21:27; ἁμαρτία/ἁμαρτίαι] ኃጢአት ፡ : 16:51, 52; 43:19; ጌጋይ ፡ : 3:20; 28:18; አበሳ ፡ : 21:24; አበሳ ፡ : 33:12;

mutandis, much the same applies in respect of the verbs, adjectives and other nouns that are cognate with ἀδικία, ἁμαρτία, ἀνομία and ἀσέβεια, with the one exception that at least within Ezekiel አበሰ ፡ ('to do wrong') is almost without exception used as the translation equivalent of ἁμαρτάνειν. It is true that within the semanitc field of sin and evil some distinctions are made. Thus for 'evil' (κακία, and the adjectives κακός and πονηρός) forms from the root አከየ ፡ are almost always used, and for πλανᾶν ('to lead astray') and πλανᾶσθαι ('to go astray') the verb ስሕት ፡ ('to go astray') is used more frequently than others.[1] But overall within the Ethiopic version distinctions within the semantic field of sin and evil are blurred, and certainly insofar as distinctions were made in the Greek Ezekiel between ἀδικία, ἁμαρτία, ἀνομία and ἀσέβεια, these have been entirely lost in the Ethiopic.

At times the switch from one translation equivalent to another occurs quite abruptly within a short passage, and this makes the problem of lack of consistency the more difficult to explain. For example, in Dan. 11:10–13, that is within the space of four verses, the word ὄχλος ('multitude') is used five times, in each case corresponding to Hebrew המון. In the Old Ethiopic text of this passage three different words are used for ὄχλος: አሕዛብ ፡ (literally 'people' or 'peoples'), which is used for the first, second and fourth occurrences, ሰብእ ፡ (literally 'men'), which is used for the third occurrence, and

---

ἀνομία/ἀνομίαι] ዓመፃ ፡ ፡ 3:19; 7:23; 8:17a; 18:20, 21; ጌጋይ ፡ ፡ 11:18; 18:24; 33:12; ኃጢአ ፡ ፡ 18:12; 28:16; ጣዖት ፡ ('idol, apostasy'): 8:17b; ἀσέβεια/ἀσέβειαι] ዓመፃ ፡ ፡ 16:43; 18:28, 30;ጌጋይ ፡ ፡ 18:31; 21:24; 23:49; ኃጢአ ፡ ፡ 12:19; ጽልሑት ፡ ('fraud, perfidy'): 21:24. It is to be observed that it is not always clear which of the four Greek nouns was in the text used by the translator, but occurrences of ዓመፃ ፡ considerably outnumber the occurrences of all three other Ethiopic words put together as the translation-equivalent of the four Greek words.

[1] πλανᾶν/πλανᾶσθαι] ስሕት ፡ ፡ 13:10; 14:9bis, 11; 44:10vid; 48:11; ጌጋ ፡ ('to err, go wrong'): 33:12; ገጠአ ፡ ('to sin'): 34:4, 16; አግገገዎ ፡ ('to cause to go astray'): 38:4; ዐለወ ፡ ('to desert (God)') 44:15; አበሰ ፡ ('to sin, do wrong'): 48:11.

ሰራዊት ፦ (literally 'forces'), which is used for the final occurrence and is also used in this same passage as the equivalent of Greek δυνάμεις ('forces'). The switch is at its most obvious in verse 11 where the Greek 'he will raise up a great multitutde, and the multitude will be given up into his hand' has been translated as 'he will raise up many people (ኅሕዛብ ፦), and the men (ሰብአ ፦) will be given up into his hand'.[1] A similar sharp switch in the rendering of ὄχλος — this time from ሰራዊት ፦ to ኅሕዛብ ፦ — occurs in Ezek. 23:46–47.[2]

VIII

The question inevitably arises as to how, in view of the general tendency towards consistency, this diversity is to be explained. There are, I think, at least four possible factors that are relevant here.

First, although for many Greek words there was a standard equivalent that could be used in any context without difficulty, there certainly does not seem to have been any attempt by the translators to pursue consistency for its own sake, that is to use the same equivalent on every occasion, whether it was appropriate to the context or not. From this point of view, diversity of rendering seems in part to have been connected with the question of meaning on the Greek side and in part with the question of appropriateness on the Ethiopic side. The question of meaning on the Greek side is obvious enough and accounts for some of the cases of diversity, for example the basic distinction that is made in the case of διδόναι between ወሀበ ፦ ('to

---

[1] Dan. 11:11: καὶ στήσει ὄχλον πολύν, καὶ παραδοθήσεται ὁ ὄχλος ἐν χειρὶ αὐτοῦ, ወያቀውም ፦ ብዙኅ ፦ ኅሕዛብ ፦ ወይትብኅ ፦ ውስተ ፦ እዴሁ ፦ ሰብኡ ፦ .

[2] The opposite to what has just been described also occurs quite frequently, namely where the same Ethiopic word is used twice within a short passage for two different Greek words. In Ezek. 12:15, for example, ዘርወ ፦ is ued for both διασκορπίζειν and διασπείρειν, in 16:9 ኀፀበ ፦ is used for both λούειν and ἀποπλύνειν, and in 16:20–21 ሠውዐ ፦ is used for both θύειν and σφάζειν. See above, pp. 90–91.

give') and ረሀየ ፡ ('to put'). But the question of appropriateness in terms of Ethiopic usage also appears to have been of some importance in that there seem to be cases where one equivalent was instinctively used rather than another because it fitted naturally in the particular context. For example, ἀνοίγειν ('to open') is translated in Ezekiel by ርኅወ ፡ when the passage refers to the opening of the heavens, or graves, or doors, but by ከሠተ ፡ when it refers to the opening of the mouth. However, somewhat inconsistently, በፅወ ፡ is used as well as ከሠተ ፡ with reference to the opening of the mouth in Ezek. 33:22, and ከሠተ ፡ , not ርኅወ ፡ , is used of the opening of graves in Ezek. 37:12.[1] The same verb ከሠተ ፡ is also a standard equivalent for ἀποκαλύπτειν ('to reveal, uncover'), but it is of interest that four times in Ezek. 16 and 23, where the reference is to the uncovering of the shame of the unfaithful wife and of the unfaithful sisters, Oholah and Oholibah, the verb ፐዸዸ ፡ is used, possibly, it seems, because the verb is particularly used of stripping clothes off.[2]

Inconsistencies of rendering that reflect differences of meaning cannot always be distinguished from inconsistencies that reflect influence from versions other than the Greek. It will be apparent from what has been said so far in these lectures that in my view such influence was exerted, not at the time of the original translation, but rather at the time of the revision based on the Syro-Arabic version in the fourteenth century and at the time of the revision based on the Hebrew text in the fifteenth or sixteenth century. There is no doubt about the influence of the versions at this later stage, and thus it is likely that in the text as it has come down to us in manuscripts from before the sixteenth century a number of examples of inconsistency of

---

[1] ἀνοίγειν] ርኅወ ፡ : 1:1; 37:13; 44:2; 46:1bis; ከሠተ ፡ : 3:27; 16:63; 29:21; 33:22; 37:12; በፅወ ፡ II.1: 33:22.

[2] ἀποκαλύπτειν] ከሠተ ፡ : 13:14; 16:57; 21:24; 22:10; 23:18bis; ፐዸዸ ፡ : 16:36, 37; 23:10; 23:29.

rendering reflect the influence of the Syro-Arabic version.[1] However, although I do not think that influence from versions other than the Greek was a relevant factor at the time of the original translation, it is desirable to check the few Old Testament manuscripts that do date from before the mid-fourteenth century to see whether inconsistencies of rendering in them are the result of non-Greek influence.

Our concern in this lecture is, however, rather with those examples of diversity of rendering which go back to the original translation and do not involve differences of meaning in the Greek. There seem to me to be two possible causes for this kind of diversity, but these point in opposite directions: it can be argued that the translators worked instinctively and at times were casual, if not arbitrary, in their procedure, or it can be argued that they were consciously attempting, for stylistic reasons, to produce variety. Of the examples discussed earlier, the treatment of ἀναγγέλλειν, ἀποκαλύπτειν and γνωρίζειν in Daniel 2 perhaps represents the outcome of an instinctive approach, the treatment of ὄχλος in Dan. 11:10–13 and Ezek. 23:46–47 perhaps represents the outcome of a conscious attempt to produce variety.

The idea that there was a deliberate attempt to introduce variety is only really plausible where the different renderings occur in close proximity to one another, although there are plenty of examples of this, and in any case it is not clear how far avoidance of repetition, which is perhaps a mark of good English style, would necessarily have been so regarded in an Ethiopian context. It is also difficult to speak with any certainty of the intention of the translators, and we can only really describe the end-result.[2] Thus, as between the two approaches suggested above, it is often difficult to decide, and examples can easily be produced that would support either

---

[1] See, for example, the discussion of the use of ፈቁዖ : , rather than ገብአ ፡ II.1, as the equivalent of διδόναι in Ezek. 9:10 (above, p. 101).

[2] Cf. Aejmelaeus, 'Translation Technique and the Intention of the Translator', *On the Trail*, 71–72.

explanation. Two examples must suffice to illustrate this and also serve to bring this lecture to a conclusion.

Three times in Ezek. 39:12–13 it is said that the house of Israel will bury Gog and his multitude, and in all three cases the Old Greek version uses the same verb, κατορύσσειν; the verb is not used elsewhere in Ezekiel. The Ethiopic uses three different expressions, two verbs that both mean 'to dig, dig up, dig in, bury' (ደገየ፡ and ፈረ፡) and a slight paraphrase 'to dig a pit for' (ከረየ፡ በቀበረ፡ ለ). In this case the passage is of such a limited extent that the suggestion that the translator was aiming at variety seems at least possible.[1]

The word σκέπη ('shelter, protection') is used three times in Ezekiel 31 and nowhere else in Ezekiel. In verse 17 it is properly translated by a word with the same meaning (ጽላሎት፡), in verse 12 it is paraphrased by a word meaning 'dwelling', and hence perhaps 'place of shelter' (ምኀድር፡), but in verse 3 the word for 'leaves' (ቍጽል፡) is used.[2] In the last case the translator may have been influenced by the surrounding context, or the present text is corrupt. But in any case the translator adopted a casual approach here, particularly if the reading 'leaves' does go back to him.

Looking back at the evidence discussed in this lecture, there is much to be said for the view that the approach of the translators was essentially instinctive, that they used the rendering that seemed on the particular occasion naturally appropriate to them. Sometimes this approach led to more or less complete consistency, sometimes to

[1] Ezek. 39:12: καὶ κατορύξουσιν ἐκεῖ τὸν Γωγ, ወይከርዩ፡ ህየ፡ በቀበረ፡ ለጎግ፡ ('And they will dig a pit there for Gog'); 39:13: καὶ κατορύξουσιν αὐτοὺς οἶκος Ισραηλ ... καὶ κατορύξουσιν αὐτοὺς πᾶς ὁ λαὸς τῆς γῆς, ወይድሕይዎሙ፡ ቤተ፡ እስራኤል፡ ... ወይፈንሪዎሙ፡ ኵሉ፡ አሕዛብ፡ ምድር፡ .

[2] Ezek. 31:3: καὶ πυκνὸς ἐν τῇ σκέπῃ, ወጽፉቅ፡ ቍጽሉ፡ . ('and thick its leaves'); 31:12: καὶ κατέβησαν ἀπὸ τῆς σκέπης αἰτῶν πάντες οἱ λαοὶ τῶν ἐθνῶν, ወወረዱ፡ እምኀድሪሆሙ፡ ኵሎሙ፡ ሰብዊተ፡ አሕዛብ፡ ('and all the hosts of the nations came down from their dwelling'); 31:17: οἱ κατοικοῦντες ὑπὸ τὴν σκέπην αὐτοῦ, <እለ፡ > ይነብሩ፡ ታሕተ፡ ጽላሎቱ፡ .

diversity; sometimes it produced renderings that were literal, sometimes ones that were relatively, or very, free. This kind of instinctive approach could lead to casualness, it not carelessness, and to be the cause of renderings that are inadequate. But over against this, there is evidence of a careful approach, and sometimes, apparently, of a conscious attempt to produce variety.

Bibliography

Quotations from the books of the Ethiopic Old Testament given in these lectures have normally been taken from the critical editions listed in section (a) of the following bibliography. Quotations from the Ethiopic text of Ezekiel have been taken from my forthcoming edition and normally follow the orthography of the base text, BL Orient. 501. For Jeremiah I have drawn on the evidence given by Schäfers, but I have also made use of photocopies of EMML 2080 and of Berlin Peterm. II, Nachtr. 42 which I happened to have available. For the Greek Bible I have used the volumes of the Göttingen edition or, for books not yet included in this edition, Rahlfs, for the Syriac the Leiden edition, and for the Hebrew *Biblia Hebraica Stuttgartensia*.

(a) Editions of the Books of the Ethiopic Old Testament[1]

Da Bassano, F., (ed.), ብሉይ ፡ ኪዳን ፡ , 4 vols, Asmara, 1922/3–1925/6.[2]

Octateuch
Dillmann, A., *Veteris Testamenti Aethiopici Tomus Primus, sive Octateuchus Aethiopicus*, 3 fasc., Leipzig, 1853–1855.

---

[1] For the books included in the canon of the Ethiopic Old Testament, see R. W. Cowley, 'The Biblical Canon of the Ethiopian Orthodox Church today', *Ostkirchliche Studien* 23 (1974), 318–23.

[2] See above, p. 3.

Genesis

Boyd, J. Oscar, *The Octateuch in Ethiopic*. Part I: *Genesis* (Bibliotheca Abessinica III), Leiden and Princeton, 1909.

Exodus and *Leviticus*

Boyd, J. Oscar, *The Octateuch in Ethiopic*. Part II: *Exodus and Leviticus* (Bibliotheca Abessinica IV), Leiden and Princeton, 1911.

The Books of Kingdoms

Dillmann, A., *Veteris Testamenti Aethiopici Tomus Secundus, sive Libri Regum, Paralipomenon, Esdrae, Esther*. Fasc. 1: *Reg. I et II*; fasc. 2: *Reg. III et IV*, Leipzig, 1861, 1871.

Paralipomena

Grébaut, S., *Les Paralipomènes. Livres I et II: version éthiopienne* (PO xxiii.4), Paris, 1932.

Esdras b

Pereira, F. M. Esteves, *Le troisième livre de 'Ezrâ (Esdras et Néhémie canoniques): version éthiopienne* (PO xiii.5), Paris, 1919.

Esther

Pereira, F. M. Esteves, *Le livre de d'Esther: version éthiopienne* (PO ix.1), Paris, 1913.

Apocryphal Books

Dillmann, A., *Veteris Testamenti Aethiopici Tomus Quintus, quo continentur Libri Apocryphi, Baruch, Epistola Jeremiae, Tobith, Judith, Ecclesiasticus, Sapientia, Esdrae Apocalypsis, Esdrae Graecus*, Berlin, 1894.

Psalms

Ludolf, H., *Psalterium Davidis aethiopice et latine, cum duobus impressis et tribus manuscriptis codicibus diligenter collatum et emendatum*, Francofurti ad Moenum, 1701.

Proverbs

Pilkington, H. A., *A Critical Edition of the Book of Proverbs in Ethiopic*, unpublished D.Phil. thesis, Oxford, 1978.

Ecclesiastes

Mercer, S. A. B., *The Ethiopic Text of the Book of Ecclesiastes*, London, 1931.[1]

Song of Solomon

Gleave, H. C., *The Ethiopic Version of the Song of Songs*, London, 1951.

Job

Pereira, F. M. Esteves, *Le livre de Job: version éthiopienne* (PO ii.5), Paris, 1907.

Hosea

Fuhs, H. F., *Die äthiopische Übersetzung des Propheten Hosea* (BBB 38), Bonn, 1971.

Amos

Pereira, F. M. Esteves, *O livro do profeta Amós e a sua versão etiópica* (Academia das sciêncas de Lisboa: Separata de "Boletin do Segunda Classe" vol. XI), Coimbra, 1917.

Micah

Fuhs, H. F., *Die äthiopische Übersetzung des Propheten Micha* (BBB 28), Bonn, 1968.

Joel

Dillmann, A., 'Der äthiopische Text des Joel', in A. Merx, *Die Prophetie des Joel und ihre Ausleger.* Halle, 1879.

Obadiah

Bachmann, J., *Dodekapropheton Aethiopum oder die zwölf kleinen Propheten der aethiopischen Bibelübersetzung.* Heft I: *Der Prophet Obadia*, Halle, 1892.

Jonah — Malachi

Löfgren, O., *Jona, Nahum, Habakuk, Zephanja, Haggai, Sacharja und Maleachi äthiopisch* (Arbeten utgivna med understöd av Vilhelm Ekmans Universitetsfond, Uppsala, 38), Uppsala, 1930.

---

[1] But see on this edition the reviews by O. Löfgren (*Monde Oriental* 26–27 (1932, 1933), 334–45) and E. Littmann (*Orientalistische Literaturzeitung* 36/6 (1933), 373–77).

Isaiah

Bachmann, J., *Der Prophet Jesaia nach der aethiopischen Bibelübersetzung*. I. Teil: *Der aethiopische Text*; II. Teil (not seen): *Der äthiopische Text in seinem Verhältnis zur Septuaginta*, Berlin, 1893.

Jeremiah

Schäfers, J., *Die äthiopische Übersetzung des Propheten Jeremias*, Freiburg im Breisgau, 1912. [Not an edition, but an important preliminary study.]

Lamentations

Bachmann, J., *Die Klagelieder Jeremiae in der äthiopischen Bibelübersetzung*, Halle, 1893.

Ezekiel

Knibb, M. A., *The Ethiopic Text of the Book of Ezekiel* [forthcoming].

Daniel

Löfgren, O., *Die äthiopische Übersetzung des Propheten Daniel*, Paris, 1927.

1 Enoch

Knibb, M. A., with the assistance of Ullendorff, E., *The Ethiopic Book of Enoch: A new edition in the light of the Aramaic Dead Sea Fragments*. Vol. 1: *Text and Apparatus*. Vol. 2: *Introduction, Ttranslation and Commentary*, Oxford, 1978.

Jubilees

VanderKam, J. C., *The Book of Jubilees*. Vol. 1: *Critical Text*; Vol. 2: *Translation* (CSCO 510–511), Leuven, 1989.

Ascension of Isaiah

Perrone, L., 'Ascensione di Isaia profeta: versione etiopica', in Bettiolo, P., Kossova, A. G., Leonardi, C., Norelli, E., and Perrone, L., *Ascensio Isaiae: Textus* (Corpus Christianorum: Series Apocryphorum 7), Turnhout, 1995, 1–129.

Paralipomena Jeremiae (4 Baruch)

Dillmann, A., 'Liber Baruch [Reliqua verborum Baruchi]', *Chrestomathia Aethiopica*, Leipzig, 1866, VIII–X, 1–15.

(b) Catalogues of Ethiopic manuscripts

The following is a list of catalogues mentioned in these lectures. For a complete list of catalogues of Ethiopic manuscripts, see R. Beylot and M. Rodinson, *Répertoire des bibliothèques et des catalogues de manuscrits éthiopiens* (Documents, études et répertoires publiés par l'Institut de Recherche et d'Histoire des Textes), Paris and Turnhout, 1995.[1]

Conti Rossini, C., 'Notice sur les manuscrits éthiopiens de la collection d'Abbadie', *JA* x.19 (1912), 551–78; x.20 (1912), 5–72; x.20 (1912), 449–94; xi.2 (1913), 5–64; xi.6 (1915), 189–238; xi.6 (1915), 445–93.

Dillmann, A., *Catalogus Codicum Manuscriptorum Bibliothecae Bodleianae Oxoniensis*. Pars VII: *Codices Aethiopici*, Oxford, 1848.

Getatchew Haile, see Macomber, W. F.

Hammerschmidt, E., *Äthiopische Handschriften vom Tânâsee 1: Reisebericht und Beschreibung der Handschriften in dem Kloster des heiligen Gabriel auf der Insel Kebrân* (VOHD XX/1), Wiesbaden, 1973.

Hammerschmidt, E., *Äthiopische Handschriften vom Tânâsee 2: Die Handschriften von Dabra Mâryâm und von Rêmâ* (VOHD XX/2), Wiesbaden, 1977.

Hammerschmidt, E., and Six, V., *Äthiopische Handschriften 1: Die Handschriften der Staatsbibliothek Preussischer Kulturbesitz* (VOHD XX/4), Wiesbaden, 1983.

Löfgren, O., *Katalog über die äthiopischen Handschriften in der Universitätsbibliothek Uppsala. Sowie Anhänge über äthiopiscshe Handschriften in anderen Bibliotheken und in Privatbesitz in Schweden* (Acta Bibliothecae R. Universitatis Upsaliensis, vol. XVIII), Uppsala, 1974.

---

[1] See also the list given by Roger Cowley in *Ethiopian Biblical Interpretation*, 419–31.

Macomber, W. F., and Getatchew Haile, *A Catalogue of Ethiopian Manuscripts microfilmed for the Ethiopian Manuscript Microfilm Library, Addis Ababa, and for the Hill Monastic Manuscript Library, Collegeville*, vol. I–, Collegeville, Minnesota, 1975–. Volumes I–III (1975, 1976, 1978) were compiled by Macomber, volume IV (1979) by Getatchew Haile, volumes V–VII (1981, 1982, 1983) by Getatchew Haile and Macomber, volumes VIII–X (1985, 1987, 1993) by Getatchew Haile.

Macomber, W. F., *Catalogue of Ethiopian Manuscripts from Abbâ Garimâ, Asatan (Church of St. Mary), Axum (Church of Zion) ... from microfilms in the collection of Dr. Donald Davies, De Land, Florida and Godfrey, Ontario, and of the Hill Monastic Manuscript Library, St. John's University, Collegeville, Minnesota*, Privately reproduced, Collegeville, Minnesota, 1979.

Six, V., *Äthiopische Handschriften 2: Die Handschriften der Bayerischen Staatsbibliothek*, herausgegeben von E. Hammerschmidt (VOHD XX/5), Wiesbaden, 1989.

Six, V., *Äthiopische Handschriften. Teil 3: Handschriften Deutscher Bibliotheken, Museen und aus Privatbesitz*, herausgegeben von E. Hammerschmidt (VOHD XX/6), Wiesbaden, 1994.

Strelcyn, S., *Catalogue of Ethiopic Manuscripts in the John Rylands University Library of Manchester*, Manchester, 1974.

Strelcyn, S., *Catalogue des manuscrits éthiopiens de l'Accademia Nazionale dei Lincei, Fonds Conti Rossini et Fonds Caetani 209, 375, 376, 377, 378* (Accademia Nazionale dei Lincei. Indici e sussidi bibliografici della bibliotheca 9), Rome, 1976.

Strelcyn, S., *Catalogue of Ethiopian Manuscripts in the British Library acquired since the year 1877*, London, 1978.

Ullendorff, E., and Wright, S. G., *Catalogue of Ethiopian Manuscripts in the Cambridge University Library*, Cambridge, 1961.

Wright, W., *Catalogue of the Ethiopic Manuscripts in the British Museum acquired since the year 1847*, London, 1877.

Zotenberg, H., *Catalogue des manuscrits éthiopiens (gheez et amharique) de la Bibliothèque Nationale*, Paris, 1877.

(c) Works of reference

Dillmann, A., *Lexicon linguae aethiopicae*, Leipzig, 1865 (reprinted New York, 1955).

Dillmann, A., *Ethiopic Grammar*, 2nd edition, London, 1907 (reprinted Amsterdam, 1974).

Leslau, W., *Comparative Dictionary of Ge'ez (Classical Ethiopic)*, Wiesbaden, 1987.

Lust, J., Eynikel, E., and Hauspie, K., *A Greek-English Lexicon of the Septuagint*, 2 vols, Stuttgart, 1992, 1996.

Prätorius, F., *Aethiopische Grammatik*, Berlin, 1886 (reprinted New York, 1955).

Thackeray, H. St John, *A Grammar of the Old Testament in Greek according to the Septuagint*, vol. I: *Introduction, Orthography and Accidence*, Cambridge, 1909.

Uhlig, S., *Äthiopische Paläographie* (AF 22), Stuttgart, 1988.

(d) Other works

Aejmelaeus, A., *On the Trail of the Septuagint Translators*, Kampen, 1993.

Amidon, P. R., *The Church History of Rufinus of Aquileia, Books 10 and 11*, New York, 1997.

Barr, J., *The Typology of Literalism in ancient biblical translations* (MSU XV = Nachrichten der Akademie der Wissenschaften in Göttingen, Phil.-Hist. Klasse, 1979, Nr. 11), Göttingen, 1979.

Barr, J., 'Words for Love in Biblical Greek', in L. D. Hurst and N. T. Wright (eds), *The Glory of Christ in the New Testament: Studies in Christology in Memory of George Bradford Caird*, Oxford, 1987, 3–18.

Bernand, E., Drewes, A. J., Schneider, R., Anfray, F., *Recueil des inscriptions de l'Éthiopie des périodes pré-axoumite et axoumite*, 2 vols, Paris, 1991.

Black, M., *The Book of Enoch or I Enoch* (Studia in Veteris Testamenti Pseudepigrapha 7), Leiden, 1985.

Brakmann, H., *Die Einwurzelung der Kirche im spätantiken Reich von Aksum*, Bonn, 1994.

Brock, S. P., 'Aspects of Translation Technique in Antiquity', *Greek, Roman and Byzantine Studies* 20 (1979), 69–87.

Brock, S. P., 'Bibelübersetzungen I.2: Die Übersetzungen des Altes Testaments ins Griechische', *TRE* 6 (1980), 163–72.

Brock, S. P., 'Bibelübersetzungen I.8: Die Übersetzungen ins Äthiopische. 2: Altes Testament', *TRE* 6 (1980), 206–7.

Brock, S. P., *Syriac Perspectives on Late Antiquity*, London, 1984.

Brock, S. P., 'Translating the Old Testament', in D. A. Carson and H. G. M. Williamson (eds), *It is Written: Scripture Citing Scripture. Essays in Honour of Barnabas Lindars, SSF*, Cambridge, 1988, 87–98.

Budge, Sir E. A. Wallis, *The Book of the Saints of the Ethiopian Church*, 4 vols, Cambridge, 1928.

Cerulli, E., *Etiopi in Palestina: Storia della comunità etiopica di Gerusalemme*, 2 vols, Rome, 1943, 1947.

Cerulli, E., *Storia della letteratura etiopica*, Milan, 1956.

Charles, R. H., 'Ethiopic Version', Hasting's *Dictionary of the Bible* I (1898), 791–93.

Charles, R. H., *The Ethiopic Version of the Book of Enoch* (Anecdota Oxoniensia, Semitic Series XI), Oxford, 1906.

Collins, J. J., 'The Son of Man in First-Century Judaism', *New Testament Studies* 38 (1992), 448–66.

Conti Rossini, C.,'Sulla versione e sulla revisione delle sacre scritture in etiopico', *ZA* 10 (1895), 236–41.

Conti Rossini, C., 'L'omilia di Yohannes, vescovo d'Aksum, in onore di Garimâ', *Actes du onzième congrès international des orientalistes, Paris — 1897*, Quatrième section, Paris, 1898, 139–77.

Conti Rossini, C., 'Note per la storia letteraria abissina', *RRAL*, ser. v, vol. 8 (1899), 197–220, 263–85.

Conti Rossini, C., 'L'evangelo d'oro di Dabra Libânos', *RRAL*, ser. v, vol. 10 (1901), 177–201.

Conti Rossini, C., *Ricordi di un soggiorno in Eritrea*, fasc. I, Asmara, 1903.

Conti Rossini, C., *Vitae sanctorum antiquiorum*. I: *Acta Yared et Pantalewon* (CSCO, Script. Aeth. ii.17, Textus, Versio), Rome, 1904.

Conti Rossini, C., *Storia d'Etiopia*. Parte prima: *Dalle origini all'avvento della Dinastia Salomonide*, Bergamo, 1928.

Conti Rossini, C., 'L'iscrizione etiopica di Ham', *Atti della Reale Accademia d'Italia*, ser. vii, vol. 1 Rome 1939, 1–14.

Conti Rossini, C., 'La leggenda di Abbâ Afsê in Etiopia', *Mélanges Syriens offerts à Monsieur René Dussaud ... par ses amis et ses élèves*, vol. i, Paris, 1939, 151–56.

Cornill, C. H., *Das Buch des Propheten Ezechiel*, Leipzig, 1886.

Cowley, R. W., 'The Biblical Canon of the Ethiopian Orthodox Church today', *Ostkirchliche Studien* 23 (1974), 318–23.

Cowley, R., *Ethiopian Biblical Interpretation: A Study in Exegetical Tradition and Hermeneutics* (University of Cambridge Oriental Publications 38), Cambridge, 1988.

Davies, D. M., 'The Dating of Ethiopic Manuscripts', *JNES* 46 (1987), 287–307.

Dillmann, A., 'Äthiopische Bibelübersetzung', *RE*[2] I (1877), 203–06.

Dogniez, C., *Bibliography of the Septuagint — Bibliographie de la Septante (1970–1993)* (Supplements to Vetus Testamentum 60), Leiden, New York, Köln, 1995.

Drewes, A. J., *Inscriptions de l'Éthiopie antique*, Leiden, 1962.

Gehman, H. S., Review of S. A. B. Mercer, *The Ethiopic Text of the Book of Ecclesiastes*, in *JAOS* 52 (1932), 260–63.

Getatchew Haile, 'The Homily in Honour of St. Frumentius, Bishop of Axum', *Analecta Bollandiana* 97 (1979), 309–18.

Getatchew Haile, 'A Text on the Saints of Kädiḥ', in Taddese Beyene (ed.), *Proceedings of the Eighth International Conference of Ethiopian Studies, University of Addis Ababa, 1984*, vol. 1, Addis Ababa, 1988, 653–64.

Getatchew Haile, 'The Homily of Abba Eleyas, Bishop of Aksum, on Mätta'', *Analecta Bollandiana* 108 (1990), 29–47.

Getatchew Haile and Misrak Amare, *Beauty of the Creation* (ሥነ ፍጥረት፡) (JSS Monograph 16), Manchester, 1991.

Getatchew Haile, *The Mariology of Emperor Zär'a Ya'eqob of Ethiopia* (Orientalia Christiana Analecta 242), Rome, 1992.

Gildemeister, J., Letter to C. R. Gregory of 20 April 1882, printed in Gregory, *Novum Testamentum Graece* (ed. C. Tischendorf), 8th edn, vol. 3: *Prolegomena*, 1894, 895–97.

Graf, G., *Geschichte der christlichen arabischen Literatur*. Band I: *Die Übersetzungen* (Studi e Testi 118), Città del Vaticano, 1944.

Grébaut, S., 'L'age du ms. éth. n⁰ 32 de Paris (Bibliothèque Nationale)', *Aethiops* 4 (1931), 9–11.

Guidi, I., 'Le traduzioni degli Evangelii in arabo e in etiopico', *MRAL*, ser. iv, vol. 4 (1888), 5–37.

Guidi, I., 'Il "Gadla 'Aragâwi"', *MRAL*, ser. v, vol. 2 (1894 (1896)), 54–96.

Guidi, I., *Le Synaxaire éthiopien*. I–III (PO i.5; vii.3; ix.4), Paris, 1906, 1909, 1912.

Guidi, I., 'La chiesa abissina' *Oriente Moderno* 2 (1922/23), 123–28, 186–90, 252–56.

Guidi, I., *Storia della letteratura etiopica*, Rome, 1932.

Hackspill, L., 'Die äthiopische Evangelienübersetzung (Math. I–X)', *ZA* 11 (1896), 117–96, 367–88.

Heider, A., *Die aethiopische Bibelübersetzung*, Leipzig, 1902.

Hofmann, J., 'Limitations of Ethiopic in Representing Greek'; see Metzger, *The Early Versions of the New Testament*, 240–56.

Honigmann, E., *Évêques et Évêchés monophysites d'Asie antérieure au VIe siècle* (CSCO 127, Subs. 2), Leuven, 1951.

Hooker, M. D., *The Son of Man in Mark*, London, 1967.

Hussey, R., *Socratis Scholastici Ecclesiastica Historia*, 3 vols, Oxford, 1853.

Knibb, M. A., 'Hebrew and Syriac Elements in the Ethiopic Version of Ezekiel?', *JSS* 33 (1988), 11–35.

Knibb, M. A., 'The Ethiopic Text of Ezekiel and the Excerpts in *GEBRÄ ḤEMAMAT*', *JSS* 34 (1989), 443–58.

Knibb, M. A., Review of S. Uhlig, *Äthiopische Paläographie*, in *ZDMG* 141 (1991), 405–408.

Knibb, M. A., Review of R. Zuurmond, *Novum Testamentum aethiopice: The Synoptic Gospels*. Part I: *General Introduction*. Part II: *The Gospel of Mark*, in *BSOAS* 55 (1992), 124–26.

Knibb, M. A., 'Messianism in the Pseudepigrapha in the Light of the Scrolls', *Dead Sea Discoveries* 2 (1995), 165–84.

Knibb, M. A., Review of S. Uhlig and H. Maehlum, *Novum Testamentum aethiopice: Die Gefangenschaftsbriefe*, in *BSOAS* 59 (1996), 203–205.

Knibb, M. A., 'The Ethiopic Translation of the Psalms', in A. Aejmelaeus and U. Quast (eds), *Der Septuaginta-Psalter und seine Tochterübersetzungen. Symposium in Göttingen 1997* (MSU XXIV), Göttingen [forthcoming].

van Lantschoot, A., 'Abbâ Salâmâ, métropolite de'Éthiopie (1348–1388) et son rôle de traducteur', *Atti del Convegno Internazionale di Studi Etiopici (Roma, 2–4 aprile 1959)* (Accademia Nazionale dei Lincei, Problemi attuali di scienza e di cultura, Quaderno N. 48), Rome, 1960, 397–401.

Lee, J. A. L., 'Equivocal and Stereoptyped Renderings in the LXX', *RB* 87 (1980), 104–17.

Littmann, E., 'Geschichte des äthiopische Litteratur', in C.
    Brockelmann et al., *Geschichte der christlichen Litteraturen
    des Orients* (Die Litteraturen des Ostens in Einzeldarstellungen
    vii.2), Leipzig, 1907, 185–270, 277–81.

Littmann, E., Review of S. A. B. Mercer, *The Ethiopic Text of the
    Book of Ecclesiastes*, in *Orientalistische Literaturzeitung* 36/6
    (1933), 373–77.

Löfgren, O., 'Die äthiopische Bibelausgabe der katholische Mission,
    mit einer Kollation des Danieltextes,' *Monde Oriental* 23
    (1929), 174–80.

Löfgren, O., Review of S. A. B. Mercer, *The Ethiopic Text of the
    Book of Ecclesiastes*, in *Monde Oriental* 26–27 (1932, 1933),
    334–45.

Löfgren, O., 'The Necessity of a Critical Edition of the Ethiopian
    Bible', in *Proceedings of the Third International Conference of
    Ethiopian Studies, Addis Ababa, 1966*, vol. 2, Addis Ababa,
    1970, 157–61.

Ludolf, H., *Commentarius ad suam Historiam Aethiopicam*,
    Francofurti ad Moenum, 1691.

Macomber, W. F., 'Two New Projects for Microfilming Oriental
    Manuscripts', in W. Voigt (ed.), *XVIII. Orientalistentag vom 1.
    bis 5. Oktober 1972 in Lübeck: Vorträge* (ZDMG Supplement
    II), Wiesbaden, 1974, 82–86.

Macomber, W. F., 'The Present State of the Microfilm Collection of
    the Ethiopian Manuscript Microfilm Library', in G. Goldenberg
    (ed.), *Ethiopian Studies: Proceedings of the Sixth International
    Conference, Tel Aviv, 14–17 April 1980*, Rotterdam, 1986,
    389–96.

Marquis, G., 'Word-Order as a Criterion for the Evaluation of
    Translation Technique in the LXX and the Evaluation of Word-
    Order Variants as Exemplified in LXX-Ezekiel', *Textus* 13
    (1986), 59–84.

Marquis, G., 'Consistency of Lexical Equivalents as a Criterion for
    the Evaluation of Translation Technique as Exemplified in the

LXX of Ezekiel', in C. E. Cox (ed.), *VI Congress of the International Organization for Septuagint and Cognate Studies, Jerusalem 1986* (SCS 23), Atlanta, 1987, 405–24.

Marrassini, P., 'Some Considerations on the Problem of the "Syriac Influences" on Aksumite Ethiopia', JES 23 (1990), 35–46.

Meinardus, O. F. A., 'The Ethiopians in Jerusalem', *Zeitschrift für Kirchengeschichte* 76 (1965), 112–47.

Meinardus, O. F. A., *Christian Egypt: Faith and Life*, Cairo, 1970.

Metzger, B. M., *The Early Versions of the New Testament: Their Origin, Transmission, and Limitations*, Oxford, 1977.

Miles, J. R., *Retroversion and Text Criticism: The Predictability of Syntax in an Ancient Translation from Greek to Ethiopic* (SCS 17), Chico, 1985.

Müller, W. W., 'Zwei weitere Bruchstuecke der Aethiopischen Inschrift aus Mârib', *Neue Ephemeris für Semitische Epigraphik* 1 (1972), 59–74, Plates VIII–IX.

Munro-Hay, S., *Aksum: An African Civilisation of Late Antiquity*, Edinburgh, 1991.

Munro-Hay, S., *Ethiopia and Alexandria: The Metropolitan Episcopacy of Ethiopia* (Bibliotheca nubica et aethiopica 5), Warsaw and Wiesbaden, 1997.

Nöldeke, T., 'Lehnwörter in und aus dem Äthiopischen', *Neue Beiträge zur semitischen Sprachwissenschaft*, Strassburg, 1910, 31–66.

Olofsson, S., *The LXX Version: A Guide to the Translation Technique of the Septuagint* (Coniectanea Biblica, Old Testament Series 30), Stockholm, 1990.

Olofsson, S., 'Consistency as a Translation Technique', *Scandinavian Journal of the Old Testament* 6 (1992), 14–30.

Phillipson, D. W., *Ancient Ethiopia. Aksum: Its Antecedents and Successors*, London, 1998.

Piovanelli, P., 'Sulla *Vorlage* aramaica dell'Enoch etiopico', *Studi Classici e Orientali* (Pisa) 37 (1987), 545–94.

Polotsky, H. J., 'Aramaic, Syriac, and Ge'ez', *JSS* 9 (1964), 1–10.

Prätorius, F., 'Äthiopische Bibelübersetzungen', RE^3 3 (1897), 87–90.

Rahlfs, A., *Studie über den griechischen Text des Buches Ruth* (MSU III.2 = Nachrichten von der Königl. Gesellschaft der Wissenschaften zu Göttingen, Phil.-Hist. Klasse, 1922), Göttingen, 1922.

Rahlfs, A., *Septuaginta–Studien I–III*, 2. Auflage, Göttingen, 1965.

Raineri, O., '"Gadla Ṣadqan" o "Vita dei Giusti": Missionari dell'Etiopia nel sesto secolo', *Nikolaus* 6 (1978), 143–63.

Raineri, O., '"Vita dei Giusti". Missionari dell'Etiopia nel sesto secolo: varianti e inno,' *Ephemerides Carmeliticae* 31 (1980), 377–413.

Raineri, O., *Atti di Habta Mâryâm (†1497) e di Iyâsu (†1508), Santi Monaci Etiopici* (Orientalia Christiana Analecta 235), Rome, 1990.

Rodinson, M., 'Sur la question des "influences juives" en Éthiopie', *JSS* 9 (1964), 11–19.

Rodinson, M., Review of E. Ullendorff, *The Ethiopians: An Introduction to Country and People*, in *Bibliotheca Orientalis* 21 (1964), 238–45.

Rodinson, M., Review of E. Ullendorff, *Ethiopia and the Bible*, in *JSS* 17 (1972), 166–70.

Schneider, R., 'Une page du Gadla Ṣâdqân', *Annales d'Ethiopie* 5 (1963), 167–69.

Schneider, R., 'Trois nouvelles inscriptions royales d'Axoum', *IV Congresso Internazionale di Studi Etiopici* (Accademia Nazionale dei Lincei, Problemi attuali di scienza e di cultura, Quaderno N. 191), Rome, 1974, Tomo I, 767–86, plates I–X.

Schwartz, E., and Mommsen, T., *Eusebius Werke* (GCS), II.1–3: *Die Kirchengeschichte*, Leipzig, 1903–09.

Sergew Hable Selassie, 'New Historical Elements in the "Gedle Aftse"', *JSS* 9 (1964), 200–203.

Sergew Hable Sellassie, *Ancient and Medieval Ethiopian History to 1270*, Addis Ababa, 1972.

Soisalon-Soininen, I., *Die Infinitive in der Septuaginta* (AASF B 132,1), Helsinki, 1965.

Soisalon-Soininen, I., *Studien zur Septuaginta-Syntax*. Zu seinem 70. Geburtstag am 4. Juni 1987 herausgegeben von A. Aejmelaeus and R. Sollamo (AASF B 237), Helsinki, 1987.

Strelcyn, S., 'Les manuscrits éthiopiens de quelques bibliothèques européens décrits récemment,' *IV Congresso Internazionale di Studi Etiopici* (Accademia Nazionale dei Lincei, Problemi attuali di scienza e di cultura, Quaderno N. 191), Rome, 1974, Tomo II, 7–61.

Szymusiak, J.-M., *Athanase d'Alexandrie: Deux apologies: à l'Empereur Constance; pour sa fuite* (SC 56bis), Paris, 1987.

Taddesse Tamrat, *Church and State in Ethiopia, 1270–1527* (Oxford Studies in African Affairs), Oxford, 1972.

Tov, E., 'Transliterations of Hebrew Words in the Greek Versions of the Old Testament: A Further Characteristic of the *kaige*-Th. Revision?', *Textus* 8 (1973), 78–92.

Tov, E., 'Three Dimensions of LXX Words', *RB* 83 (1976), 529–44.

Tov, E., 'Did the Septuagint Translators always Understand their Hebrew Text?', in A. Pietersma and C. Cox (eds), *De Septuaginta: Studies in Honour of John William Wevers on his Sixty-fifth Birthday*, Mississauga, Ontario, 1984, 53–70.

Tov, E.,'The Nature and Study of the Translation Technique of the LXX in the Past and Present', in C. E. Cox (ed.), *VI Congress of the International Organization for Septuagint and Cognate Studies, Jerusalem 1986* (SCS 23), Atlanta, 1987, 337–59.

Tov, E., *The Text-Critical Use of the Septuagint in Biblical Research* (Jerusalem Biblical Studies 8), Second edition, revised and enlarged, Jerusalem, 1997.

Tov, E., and B. G. Wright, 'Computer-Assisted Study of the Criteria for Assessing the Literalness of Translation Units in the LXX', *Textus* 12 (1985), 149–87

Uhlig, S., and Maehlum, H., *Novum Testamentum aethiopice: Die Gefangenschaftsbriefe* (AF 33), Stuttgart, 1993.

Ullendorff, E., 'An Aramaic "Vorlage" of the Ethiopic Text of Enoch?', *Atti del Convegno Internazionale di Studi Etiopici (Roma, 2–4 aprile 1959)* (Accademia Nazionale dei Lincei, Problemi attuali di scienza e di cultura, Quaderno N. 48), Rome, 1960, 259–68.

Ullendorf, E., 'Hebraic–Jewish Elements in Abyssinian (Monophysite) Christianity', *JSS* 1 (1956), 216–56 (reprinted with additions and corrections in *Studia Aethiopica et Semitica* (AF 24), Stuttgart, 1987, XI–XII, 2–42).

Ullendorff, E., *Ethiopia and the Bible* (The Schweich Lectures of the British Academy, 1967), London, 1968.

Ullendorff, E., *The Ethiopians: An Introduction to Country and People*, 3rd edition, London, Oxford, New York, 1973.

Ullendorff, E., 'Hebrew, Aramaic and Greek: the Versions underlying Ethiopic Translations of Bible and Intertestamental Literature', in G. Rendsburg et al. (eds), *The Bible World: Essays in Honour of Cyrus H. Gordon*, New York, 1980, 249–57 (reprinted in *Studia Aethiopica et Semitica* (AF 24), Stuttgart, 1987, 43–51).

Ullendorff, E., 'Hebrew Elements in the Ethiopic Old Testament', *Jerusalem Studies in Arabic and Islam* 9 (1987), 42–50.

Ullendorff, E., Review of S. Uhlig, *Äthiopische Paläographie*, in *JSS* 36 (1991), 128–34.

VanderKam, J., and Milik, J. T., 'Jubilees', in H. Attridge and others, *Qumran Cave 4.VIII: Parabiblical Texts, Part 1* (Discoveries in the Judaean Desert 13), Oxford, 1994, 1–140.

Vööbus, A., *Die Spuren eines älteren äthiopischen Evangelientextes im Lichte der literarischen Monumente* (Papers of the Estonian Theological Society in Exile 2), Stockholm, 1951.

Vööbus, A., *Early Versions of the New Testament: Manuscript Studies* (Papers of the Estonian Theological Society in Exile 6), Stockholm, 1954.

Witakowski, W., 'Syriac Influences in Ethiopian Culture', *Orientalia Suecana* 28–29 (1989–90), 191–202.

Wolska–Conus, W., *Cosmas Indicopleustès: Topographie chrétienne*, 3 vols (SC 141, 159, 197), Paris, 1968–73.

Wright, B. G., 'The Quantitative Representation of Elements: Evaluating "Literalism" in the LXX', in C. E. Cox (ed.), *VI Congress of the International Organization for Septuagint and Cognate Studies, Jerusalem 1986* (SCS 23), Atlanta, 1987, 311–35.

Wright, B. G., *No Small Difference: Sirach's Relationship to its Hebrew Parent Text* (SCS 26), Atlanta, 1989.

Ziegler, J., *Septuaginta. Vetus Testamentum Graecum Auctoritate Academiae Scientiarum Gottingensis editum.* Vol. XV: *Ieremias, Baruch, Threni, Epistula Ieremiae*, 2. Auflage, Göttingen, 1976.

Ziegler, J., *Septuaginta. Vetus Testamentum Graecum Auctoritate Academiae Scientiarum Gottingensis editum.* Vol. XVI,1: *Ezechiel*, 2. Auflage, Göttingen, 1977.

Zuurmond, R., *Novum Testamentum Aethiopice: The Synoptic Gospels.* Part I: *General Introduction.* Part II: *Edition of the Gospel of Mark* (AF 27), Stuttgart, 1989.

Index of Biblical References

Entries may cover more than one reference to the same passage on the same page.

Index of Modern Authors

Entries may cover more than one reference to the same author on the same page.

Index of Names and Subjects